THREE BRAS

The Story of the Irish Pawnshop

Jim Fitzpatrick has a keen interest in Irish social
and economic history. A regular contributor
to newspapers, magazines, radio and TV,
he is working on his next book.

Below the worn rooftops,
Upon the drab walls,
Facing the bawdy taverns,
Hang three brass balls.
There I must linger
When I cannot pay my way,
Pawning borrowed pledges
To help me through the day.

Jim Fitzpatrick

THREE BRASS BALLS

The Story of the Irish Pawnshop

Jim Fitzpatrick

The Collins Press

Published in 2001 by
The Collins Press
West Link Park
Doughcloyne
Wilton
Cork

© 2001 Jim Fitzpatrick

British Library Cataloguing in Publication data.

Typesetting by The Collins Press

Printed in Spain by Estudios Graficos ZURE

ISBN: 1-898256-10-1

CONTENTS

This book is dedicated to
the three golden girls of my life,
Marcella, Catherine and Aileen

PREFACE

Of all the trades practised in Ireland over the last number of centuries, few have had as much impact on the general populace as pawnbroking. In that time the pawnshop seems to have been under constant scrutiny. Lawmakers, lawbreakers, those with plenty of money and those with none have taken an interest in the activities of the profession. The pawnbroker has been either cherished or despised, ridiculed or admired. Yet there is no denying the pivotal role he played in the lives of many. It is no exaggeration to say that he was, until recently, as important as the highly-respected priest, doctor or teacher, the traditional pillars of society.

The reason for this is straightforward. The pawnbroker gave what many more could or would not give – instant material assistance without which many families would simply have gone hungry. Yet the pawnshop has received scant attention from Irish historians. Existing work on pawnbroking is either brief or focuses upon one specific location. There has been a need for a study of the subject on a national basis. I have attempted, in a small way, to redress this situation, not least because, as I write, there are but four pawnshops trading in the Republic of Ireland (all in Dublin), with a further two in Northern Ireland (both in Belfast): six on the entire island. Compare this to 1964, when there were 32 in the Republic alone, fourteen in Dublin and ten in Cork. These figures pale into insignificance again in relation to a century earlier when hundreds were active up and down Ireland.

In most places, the pawnshop is now but a memory. Places like Pawnbroker Lane in Ballina and Pawn Office Lane in Killarney are rare public reminders of a business that was once as

1

A relic of days gone by – Pawn Office Lane, Killarney, County Kerry.

commonplace as the butcher's or corner shop.

Is pawnbroking dying in Ireland? For generations, the prophets of doom, perhaps with the best intentions in the world, have gleefully rubbed their hands and predicted the extinction of a type of business that symbolised poverty and misery for generations. If the pawnshop were gone, they argued, this would be an indication that the economic condition of our country was better than hitherto, that the bad old days were consigned to history. Yet at this period of Ireland's development, as the door has opened to the twenty-first century, the absolute and widespread poverty of the past seems to behind us, the Celtic Tiger is roaring, the government coffers are overflowing, and most of us are better off materially, if not spiritually. But has the pawnshop gone? We must answer in the negative. What about when our economy is not so good, as inevitably it will be some day? Will we see the opening up of more pawnshops? Perhaps, but by the same token, the last of our pawnshops could close its doors overnight, and pawnbroking would suddenly be an extinct trade within these shores. To allow this to happen without any effort to record its story in Ireland would be a terrible pity.

Without doubt, the pawnbroker has rarely been given due respect and praise. Records clearly show there was a stigma attached to the activity for hundreds of years, something which has been very hard to shake off. This negative attitude is illustrated by a writer to the *Cork Constitution* newspaper in July 1828, who wrote:

> It is really most comical to witness efforts of the miserable faction that is disturbing the peace of this country, with their public meetings and resolutions. Here you will see pawnbrokers ... assuming to themselves the appellation of 'esquires'. What a state of society we live in when men who are respectable enough in their own sphere of life cannot keep themselves so, but must intrude on the public and lay themselves open to the laughter and contempt of every man of intellect.

In October 1860, a correspondent to another daily newspaper, in a reference to members of Dublin Corporation, complained of 'a cabal of ... pawnbrokers ... who derive a sordid livelihood by ministering to the meanest wants of mankind'.

Until quite recently, the pawnbroker was not readily accepted by the wealthier classes as an equal. To them, he was not a 'real' businessman in his own right, not like the banker or merchant. Even historians seem to have been anxious to elevate banking to a much higher level, though at one stage there was little or no difference. Charles McCarthy-Collins, in *The law and practice of banking in Ireland*, published in 1880, stated:

> It is not usual in Ireland for a banker in ordinary transactions to accept a deposit of

It's farewell to this pawnshop at Sullivan's Quay, Cork, as new owners get out the paint.

goods as security for advances, for not alone would such a practice be inconvenient and troublesome, but, further, it would *degrade* banking to the *low level* of pawnbroking.

The majority of the pawnbroker's customers, being poor or destitute, and thus materially on a rung of the ladder of society beneath him, perhaps felt that he was not quite 'one of our own'. The pawnbroker was thus in a type of limbo, amongst the people, but separate. And yet, conversely, the pawnshop was widely known as 'the poor man's bank' (a title incidentally the Agricultural Bank tried to claim in 1835), implying, in no uncertain manner, its importance for the needy.

This book is not intended as a tribute to pawnbrokers. I have written as an observer, from a distance, with no vested interest or background in pawnbroking. I do feel, however, that whatever their past perceptions, readers will find it unavoidable not to hold, if not a healthy respect, at least some respect for the owners of pawnshops, the majority of whom operated fairly and justly through difficult times and in difficult circumstances.

Although not intended to be a thorough history of the trade in

Old (wooden) golden balls from O'Keeffe's of Carrick-on-Suir, now a museum piece.

Ireland, I hope this book will be informative to all, especially those, like myself, who live in an area that has not seen a pawnshop for many years. Much contained herein will be new to them. To those who still use the pawnshop, or those in the past who were as regular inside the door of 'the Uncle's' as they were at Sunday Mass, I would be happy to think they also will find much of interest within these covers.

If my book is biased in any direction, it is towards the customers who pawned as a way of life, not because they wanted to but because they had to, those same people who pawned their most precious valuables, not due to a craving for drink (to which temptation many unfortunately succumbed), but just to help their families out of whatever dire financial circumstance they found themselves in. It is these who have most of all earned my admiration in the story of the Irish pawnshop.

JIM FITZPATRICK
2001

ACKNOWLEDGEMENTS

The support of so many people was vital to the writing of this book, too numerous to mention in full, but I would in particular like to acknowledge the following:

Colin Rynne, for his unstinting support and guidance; John Brereton, Pat Carthy and Pat Kearns, pawnbrokers all, for sharing their knowledge and for allowing me to photograph inside their pawnshops; William Jones, ex-pawnbroker, for his personal insight and memories of the trade; Thomas McCarthy, poet and novelist, for his continuous and valued encouragement; Mark Tierney, OSB, for access to the Barrington Papers at Glenstal Abbey, County Limerick; James O'Keeffe, Carrick-on-Suir, for his kindness during my visit to his locality and for pawnbroking memorabelia; Séamus Ó Conaill of Galway for a pre-Famine pawn ticket; the staff of the various county and city libraries and archives depositories, in particular Ann, Kieran and Stephen at Cork City Library; the Religious Society of Friends in Ireland; thanks to D.A. Levistone Cooney for providing help regarding pawnbrokers and the Methodists in Ireland; of course, all those who allowed me tell their stories of pawnshops (they know who they are), and in so doing gave me a better understanding of the trade.

The help of my family, immediate and extended, is greatly appreciated (a special thank you for everything to Mam and Dad). Lastly, but most importantly, to my wife Marcella and our lovely daughters, Catherine and Aileen – your support and indeed patience (will you ever forget all that paper?) was vital to the completion of this book. Thanks girls. I hope the result will please you.

I would like also to thank the following for permission to reproduce their photographs: pages 36, 73 and 74 courtesy of the *Old Limerick Journal*; page 49 and 52 courtesy of the National Library of Ireland; page 27 courtesy of John Brereton; page 58 courtesy of Pat Kearns; page 39 courtesy of James O'Keeffe; page 71 courtesy of Glenstal Abbey, County Limerick; page 41 courtesy of Cork City Library; page 91 courtesy of Séamus Ó Conaill; page 108 courtesy of the *Evening Echo*, Cork; page 3 courtesy of Quay Co-Op, Cork; page 17 courtesy of Donore Credit Union, Dublin; page 23 courtesy of Dublin Corporation; page 30 courtesy of the Catholic Encyclopedia; page 33 (top) courtesy of the British Museum, London; page 33 (bottom) www.moderntimes.com/palace/chaplin/cc-image/pawnshop.jpg; page 46 courtesy of William Jones; page 34 courtesy of Pan Books, London; page 40 courtesy of Peter Pearson; page 50 courtesy of Naas Local History Group, County Kildare; I have been unable to trace the owners of the illustration on page 57 (King George III). If they would contact myself or the publishers, we shall be pleased to acknowledge them in any future edition. All other photographs, author's own collection.

Chapter One

POVERTY, A DOGGED FOE

Poverty is not a shame, but being ashamed of it is.

Thomas Fuller (1608-1661)

Poverty has been with us since ... well ... virtually since Adam and Eve. The 'haves' and the 'have-nots' have lived as uncomfortable bedfellows, yet Ireland is no stranger to abject poverty. For various reasons, there has always been a high percentage of the population on or below the bread line, barely able to eke out a basic living.

Throughout the eighteenth century, people were doing well to stay alive. Dean Swift spoke in 1727 of the:

> miserable dress and diet and dwelling of the people ... families living in filth and nastiness, without a single shoe or stocking to their feet, or a house so convenient as an English hog-sty to receive them.

This description could easily have belonged to a later time. Even two centuries on from Swift, the conditions for many had barely improved. Work, when available, was often temporary and poorly paid. Women were usually consigned to cleaning jobs or some domestic work, men almost exclusively relying upon trades or manual work. Few obtained good and long-term employment. One French visitor, Gustave de Beaumont, commented in

1839, that 'in all countries paupers may be discovered, but an entire nation of paupers is what never was seen until it was shown in Ireland.' A high percentage of the Irish population did not know where their next meal was coming from. This state of affairs ensured that the poor stayed poor, dwelling in slum-like conditions, malnourished and with few opportunities for education. Learning for them was the "hard way", out on the streets, bringing in a few pennies to feed their families. It was estimated in 1836 that nearly two and a half million people in Ireland (then about a third of the population) were destitute for most of the year. As late as 1938, a survey of Dublin tenements revealed that 60 per cent were unfit for human occupation, or, in terms of their occupants, 65,000 people in that city were living in condemned dwellings.

Outside temporary or badly paid work, what other means had people to obtain money? Social welfare payments from the Department of Social Welfare, which was established in 1947, are only a relatively recent innovation. Before that, people had to rely mostly on provisions in the *Poor Laws* of 1838, until further reforms in late Victorian times. In 1897, the *Workmen's Compensation Act* helped those injured in the course of their employment. In 1908, *Old Age Pensioners* became entitled to payments. *Children's Allowance* became available for civil servants in 1926 (after Irish independence), but most had to wait until 1944 before it became available on a wider scale. A *Widows and Orphans Pension* came into effect in 1935, whilst *Unemployment Assistance* was introduced only a couple of years earlier, in 1933. The *Wet-Time Act*, providing insurance against loss of wages due to bad weather for men working in the building and painting trades, was introduced in 1942.

Yet for large families such welfare payments hardly sufficed. People required, and were usually given, assistance from family and neighbours to help them out of financial predicaments, a fact often commented upon to this day by people recalling the neighbourliness in the streets and laneways of their youth.

Sometimes a person's loss of income could not be alleviated in

Stocks such as these were commonly used to punish beggars and thieves in the past.

such a way. A minority of women turned to prostitution: brothels were a familiar sight in the big cities. Begging was always prevalent, and some felt they had no choice but to resort to this degradation. It was a risk. Beggars faced the stocks, whipping, and prison during certain periods of our history. Arrest was a possibility, whilst assault by thugs was an omnipresent hazard.

Help had to come from other sources. There were, and still are worthy charities. The offer of charity was sometimes selective, however, particularly in earlier years, and it was not always solely for the good of the poor that these organisations were set up. Often it was to get the nuisance of beggars off the street, or to stress the privileged position of the few. Once the beggars were out of sight, and preferably in another town, their well-being was not all that important.

The *Poor Law Relief Act* of 1601 in England did not extend to Ireland and the first Poor House in Dublin was not built until a century later. This became the country's first House of Industry, in

Part of the former Foundling Hospital (now Murphys Brewery), Cork.

1730, where beggars and vagrants had a choice: either work hard, as rules instructed, or face punishment. The second House was opened in Cork in 1747 at the outskirts of Blackpool, and functioned totally as a Foundling Hospital, closing in the early 1850s. Only part of the Dublin House of Industry was reserved for foundlings. Life in the Foundling Hospitals was cruel for the young inmates – many deaths, filth, bad clothing and food, poor ventilation and incompetent management. The first working House of Industry for Cork, 'to establish an asylum for distress, and be a House of Correction for vagrancy', did not open until 1776.

Houses of Industry were established mainly to remove the idle beggars from the streets. By 1796, about 1,700 paupers were in the Dublin house, being better fed than unfortunates outside on the streets. De Latocnayne, a Frenchman, remarked in 1796 that 'their food is infinitely better than that found on the tables of the peasantry … they have meat once a week; bread, potatoes and other vegetables every day; very clean beds …' In Cork, in 1818, the daily average of persons at the House was 448, and in 1827,

3,159 received relief. Yet inmates despised having to resort to dwell in these buildings and those who were forced to enter (for upwards on four years) regularly tried to escape. Only some, those who were thought not 'idle', could come and go as they pleased.

Acts of 1772 and 1774 for the relief of the poor in Ireland did not really help in practical terms, and so for the next few decades misery and anxiety prevailed on the streets, the highways and the byways of the country. A *Poor Law Relief Act* finally came to Ireland in 1838, which led to the building of the dreaded workhouses. There were 130 unions set up

Dublin's oldest surviving charity, the Sick and Indigent Roomkeeper's Society.

around the country, and 163 workhouses built – 49 in Munster, 46 in Ulster, 40 in Leinster and 28 in Connacht. Soon, they became overcrowded, filthy and unhygienic, with many uncaring members of staff. John Mitchel wrote of the workhouses in 1848 that 'a man went in, a pauper came out'.

All but five of the workhouses were still open in 1914, with around 25,000 obtaining relief therein. The workhouse system was abolished in the 1920s, and the buildings either abandoned, gutted during the Civil War, turned into hospitals or County Homes, or eventually demolished.

Collectively, and despite their faults, these institutions – the workhouses, houses of industry, charities – and indeed the compassionate private individuals who acted selflessly against the attitudes of the times helped the worse-off in society. But many

A section of the old workhouse, Newcastlewest, 1999.

chose to stay on in the slums, too proud to end up as paupers yet too pauperised to escape. Many decided they could take no more and emigrated.

People turned to petty or more serious thieving, only to face punishment like flogging, jail, transportation and even execution, and our history books record cruel punishments for seemingly minor thefts.

Poverty was never restful. Unless one was born into the elite class or blessed with some special talent, life was a constant struggle, with little prospect of release. Whatever means possible to relieve their situation was taken by people. This sometimes meant going to a moneylender, and his was a familiar face in Ireland.

Chapter Two

THE MONEY LENDERS

If you would like to know the value of money, go try and borrow some.
Benjamin Franklin (1706-1790)

We need money. If we cannot obtain money one way, we try another. If our earnings are not enough to meet our needs, we tend to borrow.

The most common lending institutions today are banks, building societies and credit unions. Loans are sought and given for anything from mortgages to house improvements, from cars to holidays, from education courses to computers. In our lives, credit cards are arguably more common than decks of playing cards.

Banking came to Ireland many centuries ago. Italian merchants were amongst the first to practice this trade here. They are thought to have come in the twelfth century when the Normans conquered England. Bankers came from Italy to assist the invaders. Subsequently they crossed over to Ireland where they set up as collectors of papal revenues (known as Peter's Pence) and royal revenues, but also as moneylenders to the clergy, aristocracy, government and townsmen, and wool and silk merchants. Later private, but notoriously undependable, bankers opened banks around the country, which often closed overnight leaving their depositors destitute. Few were people of wealth or property, just opportunists. No licence was needed for this practice. They knew that even if their banks collapsed, they generally came out of the experience wealthier than on entering. Even shopkeepers and publicans were calling themselves bankers, and banking was quickly being brought into disrepute by swindlers and con men. Although the Bank of England was established as far back as 1694, efforts to form a Bank of Ireland, despite repeated attempts, did not succeed until 1783. By this period, banking began to settle into some level of normality and respectability. Nonetheless, all banks were to remain, for many more decades, exclusive, far out of reach of the middle to low income earners. It was to be many years before the less privileged would even be welcome inside the doorways of the main banks, let alone be considered for loans.

Charitable Loan Societies were established in Ireland early in the nineteenth century. They were, according to the preamble of an 1823 law, chiefly aimed at giving loans 'for providing implements of industry for the labouring classes of His Majesty's Subjects'. These societies were set up all over the country, with the Central Board in Dublin overseeing each branch. Whilst the Loan Societies did offer assistance, there were restrictions to the granting of loans. Not everyone fitted into the category of 'industrious classes' for whom these loans were intended. All of those unable or even, let it be said, unwilling to work, were the principal victims, and many could not procure assistance. In addition, no individual could obtain loans valued at more than £10 in one year, and on top of that, failure to repay any loan also meant criminal prosecution.

Building Societies, in the form of Friendly Societies, originated in eighteenth-century England (the oldest for which records survive dates from Birmingham in 1775) mainly, as their name implies, to help people buy or build homes. They were established in Ireland shortly afterwards. But the average person could never even contemplate such a step. By circumstance, he was far more modest in his ambitions. Regular food and clothing and a little pocket money was as far as his aspirations could reach.

The now-flourishing Credit Union movement, established originally on nineteenth-century mainland Europe,

Donore Credit Union, Ireland's first Credit Union at Donore, in Dublin.

only came to Ireland in 1958, beginning with the formation of Donore Credit Union in Dublin. The popularity of the movement soon spread. At last, people from the most stigmatised areas could obtain loans at a reasonable rate. They saved and lodged whatever they could afford regularly, obtaining a loan of double or even three times the amount of their savings, and all for the minimum amount of loan interest. The snag was that one had to be a regular saver to obtain a loan. A sudden need for money by a non-saver would, on the whole, not have been satisfied at a credit union.

Perhaps certain people facing such emergency situations could have turned to dealers. This needs explanation. A dealer, say, might operate from her home. She would sell five-pound Orders or vouchers to people, and these Orders could be cashed in at specific stores in town to buy shoes or clothing, and the dealer would have to be paid back every week with an extra payment as her profit.

Another source was the infamous moneylender. Some of these were fair and treated their customers honestly and with understanding. More, however, were like vultures, feeding off their prey. Many moneylenders undoubtedly deserved the label frequently thrown upon them – usurers. Usury, which is now generally considered to be the *overcharging* of interest on loans as against the original concept of charging *any* interest, has been regarded as one of the most despicable evils for centuries, and those who were seen to be taking improper advantage of people in need were roundly despised. Usury is and was a worldwide malaise. In the Bible, which has many references to interest and usury, St Paul says in his first letter to the Corinthians:

> You know perfectly well that people who do wrong will not inherit the kingdom of God: people of immoral lives, idolaters, adulterers, catamites, sodomites, thieves, *usurers*, drunkards, slanderers and swindlers will never inherit the kingdom of God.

In Parma, Italy, in 1477, a usurer's body was disinterred and his body dragged through the streets with contempt. Behind him followed an old woman who had been obliged to give him an egg a day in return for a ducat she had borrowed. Usurers were at that time refused a Christian burial.

For many years the Church debated the morality of charging interest, with theologians and philosophers such as Plato, Aristotle, Cicero, Luther and Zwingli against interest charges, whilst many more believed that some interest was justifiable to cover the trouble and risk faced by the lender. This moral argument went on for centuries. The Church issued many directives forbidding interest, such as at the First Council of Arles (314 AD) and at the Council of Nicea (325 AD), both aimed at clerics, and at the Council of Carthage (345AD) which extended the directive to lay people. In 1179 AD, at the Third Lateran Council, at the Council of Lyon (1274 AD), and in 1311-12 AD at the Council of Vienne, the ban was copper-fastened, with the Vienne Council going so far as to brand usurers as heretics:

> If indeed someone has fallen into the error of presuming to affirm pertinaciously that the practice of usury is not sinful, we decree that he is to be punished as a heretic.

But the arguments continued, and gradually the Church's attitude softened. Finally, at the Fifth Lateran Council (1515 –1517 AD), called by Pope Julius II but completed by his successor Leo X, the Holy See accepted the moral right of Charity Pawnshops (*Monte Pietatis*) to charge some interest on loans:

> We declare and define, with the approval of the sacred council, that the above mentioned credit organisations do not introduce any kind of evil or provide any incentive to sin if they receive, in addition to capital, a moderate sum for their expenses and by way of compensation … it is our will that all religious as well as ecclesiastical and secular persons who henceforth dare to preach or argue otherwise incur the punishment of immediate excommunication.

This opened the door for moneylenders and many, it must be stressed, plied their business without causing hardship to the peoples they served. Usury, nevertheless, was still very much in evidence, and remained globally condemned. Indeed, in the Code of Canon Law (*c.* 2345), the Church still looks harshly upon usurers.

In 1634, the Irish Parliament had passed an Act aimed at restraining usury, reducing the legal rate of interest to ten per cent. In 1704 it was further reduced to eight per cent, to seven per cent in 1721 and, in 1737, to six per cent. No doubt these efforts were aimed at people like the notorious 'banker' and usurer John Damer, who served under Cromwell and came over from England to settle in Ireland. Of the same ilk was James Southwell, whose practices forced parliament to curb all usurers activities. Laws, unfortunately, did not wipe out the practice of usury entirely, and excessive interest charges have lasted, arguably, to this day.

All of the above-mentioned private and corporate lenders offered (at a profit) finance to the poor. It cannot be denied that each, to a small or large degree, helped the recipients. Yet the most common and reliable avenue open to the masses to obtain money in time of shortage was, most probably, the pawnshop.

Chapter Three

THE PAWNSHOP: THE POOR MAN'S BANK

Money can't buy friends, but you can get a better class of enemy.
Spike Milligan (1918-)

Sometimes, wherever people turned for help, the door was firmly closed against them. Oftentimes, though, even the most needy had something, *anything* of use, whether it was an old chair or table, or a picture on the wall, or even the clothes on their backs. It was usually these seemingly valueless items that enabled them to acquire a little money. Time and time again, the needy, after another day of despair, could turn down a street knowing that there was one person before them who would not turn them away empty-handed. He was the pawnbroker. Call him what you like, they would say, but at least he will give me some form of a loan. He will take care of me. Unfortunately, this trust was not always merited. Some who accepted pawns made up their own rules. Most of these characters were not even legitimate pawnbrokers. Called 'dolly shops' (after the black wooden dolls hung outside their doors), or 'wee pawns' in Scotland, these illegal pawnbrokers took virtually everything in pawn, gave out trivial loans, charged high interest and gave very little time for the customers to redeem their pledges. They had no qualms about accepting stolen goods. Some such 'dolly shops' existed in

Ireland. Fortunately, there were still plenty of honest and legally registered pawnbrokers about, who were vital to the needs of the poor. They gave immediate material assistance. Moralising and sympathy did not put bread on the table. As Samuel Johnson mused in 1791:

> When I was a very poor fellow, I was a great arguer for the advantages of poverty ... but in a civilised society personal merit will not serve you so much as money will. Sir, you may make an experiment. Go into the street and give one man a lecture on morality and another a shilling, and see which will respect you the most.

This very much applied to pawnbrokers. They made money out of the poor, no denying that, but at least they gave when others turned away. Whatever respect came their way usually came from the very same recipients of that money.

No one knows precisely when pawning first began. It is an ancient practice going back to Biblical times. It was undertaken in the Far East as well as the West. The Chinese are known to have operated a system more than 2,000 years ago, and the ancient Greeks and Romans were just as familiar with the trade. Documents and artefacts found in China relating to the period 273 AD to 778 AD included a figurine of a dancer with arms made from 33 pawn tickets and receipts of pawned clothing.

Pawning, even when the term was probably not used, extended in ancient times to Ireland too, where pledging was an everyday occurrence for the early Irish. At that time, more than 1,000 years ago, a *gell*, meaning a pledge, could be anything from a warrior's sword to animals, a goblet, or the needle of an embroidress. A *gell* was an object of value given by its owner to another for a fixed period of time. There were several types of loans – *ón* (a loan for use), *airliciud* (a loan for consumption), *fri aircheann* (a loan for a fixed period), *fri anairchenn* (an open loan), *errech* (an enforced loan). Goods were pledged and loans given. There were sureties (the *ráth*, the *naidm*, the *aitire*) who were responsible for enforcing the contracts. To all intents and purposes it was an ancient form of pawning.

Yet a regulated trade of pawnbroking in Ireland was still a long way off.

Nearly all early records of pawning are lost, leaving us to only imagine what it was like in practice, but, from the twelfth century, we do have the odd interesting reference. In 1128, an English-born Cistercian, Abbot Stephen of Lexington, when writing to the Abbot of Citeaux from Ireland, as part of his tour of Irish monasteries, referred to the dire state of the monastery he was visiting:

> We have with us the seal of a certain abbot which was pawned in a tavern for eighteen pence, and we saw the seal of another abbot in the same manner in the possession of a secular; consequently, on account of this the monasteries are reduced almost to nothing.

By the seventeenth century, the need for ready cash could be felt by all, even by Municipal Authorities. Due to a severe shortage of coins, money was borrowed at high rates of interest. In or around 1608, a contemporary account stated:

> People of all sorts are driven to great extremity: for the better sort having occasion to take up money to serve their use are found to give to the greedy usurer £40 per £100, and that upon a pawn either of plate or land in mortgage, not daring to trust one another upon their bonds; the poorest being forced to pawn their apparel or other necessary implements wherewith they get their living and pay ordinarily for 20s. 6d. every week to their undoing.

In Cork City, in 1616, one Dominick Creagh pawned a silver goblet with John Coppinger Fitz-Adam for 40 shillings. In the same city, a year later, David Pounch Fitzpatrick pawned a silver jewel with Adam Gold and received the same amount, whilst in 1618, William Darwell pawned four locks for sixteen shillings. None of these particular pledges had been redeemed within twelve months of pawning.

Incredibly, Dublin Corporation was forced, in 1634, to pawn the City Seal. Dating from the thirteenth century, the seal fetched £1,000 from a pawnbroker.

There are other instances of pawning from surviving records. In 1641, in Limerick, one Thomas Arthur recorded: 'For said gearran

The thirteenth-century city seal of Dublin, pawned in 1634.

taken in pawne for the respett of homadge which the said Kenney fayled to pay as he was bound, I payed 01-13-6.' In 1664, Lady Dillon pawned a waistcoat belonging to Sir James Dillon in County Roscommon.

It was more than a century later again before pawning was to be governed by specific rules. Thus in the 1600s and for most of the 1700s – long before, and for at least a century after Oliver Cromwell cast a dark shadow over Ireland – the person accepting pledges could charge whatever interest he liked and could buy and sell pledges on his own terms. This inevitably led to abuse, yet paupers had no option but to pawn. They pawned their meagre possessions to feed and clothe their families, as well as to pay tithes and taxes. The practice of pawning was regularly mentioned in newspapers and reports on social conditions in the nineteenth and twentieth centuries, whether because of some crime at a pawnshop (in November 1887, a workhouse boy named Daniel Rourke was arrested for trying to pawn stolen boots at Levis' Pawnshop at Sullivan's Quay in Cork), or via observations by experts studying poverty in Ireland. An unemployed tradesman in Dublin pawned all his possessions in the early 1900s, remarking ruefully:

My own clothes are so worn that it is questionable whether I will be taken into any firm ... none of them [his wife and six children] are able to go outside the door for want of clothes. None of the children could attend school or their place of worship for the last four months.

Oftentimes, people pawned when they could least afford to. In January 1820, the poor of Cork had to pawn the bare coverings off their beds just for food, and this in the freezing winter. In Dublin in the early twentieth century, reliance on pawnshops was extensive. In 1904, Dr T.J. Stafford, medical commissioner of the Local Government Board, and C.D. La Touche jointly did a survey of 5,000 people in Dublin to ascertain a typical picture of conditions in a working class district. They reported that for many families rents were paid every Monday, and accounts were settled on Saturday with the grocer where food was obtained on tick or from money obtained at the pawnshop. They found that loans from pawnshops were necessary for survival.

Pawnbrokers were, in some ways, the best moneylenders of all. They would not, nor indeed could not, chase after their customers for failing to repay loans. Today, how many of us can say that about our borrowings?

Chapter Four

PAWNING EXPLAINED

When it is a question of money, everybody is of the same religion.

Voltaire (1694-1778)

The word pawn, according to the Oxford English Dictionary, means: 'A thing or person given, deposited or left in another's keeping, as security for a debt or for the performance of some action.'

We may raise our eyebrows at the notion of pawning people, but this apparently did happen, as when Edward III pledged the Earls of Derby as security for a loan obtained on the Continent. Dryden, in 'Cleomenes III', states: 'He must leave behind, for pawns, his mother, wife and son.'

Pawn, as a word, may have its origins in Old French, where *pan* meant pledge or security. Another possibility is the German word *pfand*, meaning much the same, or the Latin *pannus*, which is explained as a cloth or rag. Pawn in the sense of pledging rather than as a figure in chess (which originates from thirteenth-century *pehon* or *pedon*, meaning a foot-soldier), can be found in use in the English language in 1496, although 'pawnbroker' did not appear until 1637. A slang term commonly used in America, which is thought to have come from the Dutch word for prison, is *hock*, or a *hockshop*, meaning to pawn and a pawnshop respectively. A familiar term used as well, to this day indeed, is the endear-

Pat Carthy, pawnbroker, valuing a pledge.

ment *Uncle*. 'I'm off down to the Uncle', would be commonly heard.

To 'lay up in lavender' may have been an old upper-class expression for pawning, used in the sixteenth century. As one looks further afield, the term 'bottomry' sometimes occurs, that is, when a ship is pledged as security for a loan to, say, undertake a journey. From the basic word pawn we get, as well as pawnshop (the premises where pawning takes place), the term pawnbroker, that is the person who practices the trade.

Pawnshops can be a place to purchase goods at bargain prices or, more traditionally, as a source to obtain ready cash. This cash is given by way of a loan, where the customer pledges, or hands over, some item of value to the pawnbroker in return for money. The pawnbroker must keep the item for months or years depending on its value and the regulations in force in any given country at a particular time. During this period, the customer can claim back (redeem) his property (called a pledge), providing he repays the loan plus whatever fees or charges the pawnbroker levies. People also use pawnshops to offload items they no longer want. They go through the same procedure, get as much money as they can and never come back, which is perfectly legal. The pawnbroker in this situation can send the unredeemed item to auction.

The procedure of pawning is relatively simple. One approaches the clerk behind the counter of a pawnshop and shows to him the item he wishes to pledge. The clerk examines it and says how much he will give. The customer might accept his first offer or try to bargain for more (which can, by all accounts, be a humiliating experience, especially for someone not used to pawning). Once the loan amount is agreed, the clerk, probably after asking for some identification, enters the details into his

PAWNED WITH

John Brereton PAWNBROKER LTD.

No: 5370

LICENSED PAWNBROKER
108 CAPEL STREET, DUBLIN 1.   TELEPHONE: 873 0436

Date: _____

Name: _____

Address: _____

Pledge: _____

_____

Loan: _____

I	
N	
S	

1. Charges
(a) For this ticket .... Pence.

(b) Interest at the rate per calendar month.................... Pence (if the term of the loan is less than one calendar month, it will be charged for as one month. After the first calendar month, a part of a month exceeding seven days will be charged for as a month and a part of a month not exceeding seven days will not be charged for).
(c) The charge for storage of this pledge will be .... Pence per calendar moth or any part of a month.

M.P. ....

This constitutes a A.P.R. of................................ per cent if pawned/pledged for 4 months.

(up to a maximum of............................ per cent if pawned/pledged for 1 month or less)

2.THIS IS A 4 MONTHS PLEDGE.

3. After the expiration of that time the pledge may be sold by auction by the pawnbroker. But it may be redeemed by the pawner at any time before the day of sale.

4. Within twelve calendar months after the sale the pawner may, on payment of a fee of twenty five pence, inspect the account of the sale in the pawnbroker's book and in the auctioneer's catalogue and receive any surplus produced by the sale. If, however, within six months before or after that sale, the sale of another pledge or pledges of the same person has resulted in a deficit the pawnbroker is entitled to set off the deficit against the surplus.

5. If a pledge though default, neglect, or wilful misbehaviour on the part of the pawnbroker, is lost, destroyed or is of less value at the time of redemption than it was at the time of pawning, the pawner may apply to the District Court for an order of compensation. The amount of compensation, if any, awarded shall be deducted from the sum payable to the pawnbroker or as the case may require, shall be paid by the pawnbroker in such a manner as the Court may direct.

6. If the pledge is destroyed or damaged by the fire the pawnbroker, if the pawn-ticket is tendered to him before the expiry of the period within which the pledge would have been redeemable, will be bound to pay an amount equal to on half of the amount of the loan, unless otherwise agreed upon by the pawnbroker.

7. If this ticket is lost or mislaid the pawner should at once apply to the pawnbroker for a form of declaration; otherwise the pawnbroker will be bound to deliver the pledge to anyone who produces the ticket to him and claims to redeem the pledge.

8. Please insure your own property as we are not responsible for goods taken illegally from the premises of the above name company

....**Pawnbroker**

CLOSED ALL DAY WEDNESDAY ....**Pawner**

Pawning pledge used by Breretons Pawnbrokers in recent years.

books – the customer's name and address, a description of the item, and the amount of the loan – and then writes out much the same information on a numbered ticket. He attaches the ticket to the pledged item and hands the customer a duplicate. The item is then sent to the pawnbroker's stores. When the customer gets enough money together, he will come back to the pawnshop and present his ticket. The pledged item is brought from the stores and once he pays the loan interest and ticket money, the customer can take his property back.

It often happened that instead of paying out money to redeem goods, a person might pledge another item – if he did not have money to pay off the loan and costs.

The laws and practices of pawnbroking vary from country to country, but in essence they have followed the above pattern for hundreds of years. Once one sees the golden balls above the door, one generally knows what to expect inside, irrespective of territory.

Chapter Five

ALL THAT GLITTERS: THE GOLDEN BALLS

Poverty does not mean the possession of little, but the lack of much.
Antipater of Macedonia (*c.* 397-319BC)

What is the first thing that comes to our minds when we think of pawnshops?

For most of us, it is the image of the three golden balls, perched above the doorway. Normally they are made of metal, but long ago wood was frequently used. Evidence of the three golden balls in Ireland comes in an advertisement in an eighteenth-century Dublin newspaper, *Harding's Weekly Impartial Newsletter*, which ran: 'At the Three Golden Balls in Castle Street ... are to be sold a choice of fine English cloths.'

Much like the red and white striped barber-shop pole, the golden balls quickly tell us what type of trade goes on inside. It is globally and immediately recognisable.

The origin of the three golden balls makes fascinating reading.

Because pawnbroking goes back many centuries and is spread throughout the world, there is no one definitive explanation as to why the balls were chosen as a logo. Indeed, it is said that pawnbrokers only adopted this symbol in recent centuries, having previously displayed three blue bowls. The belief is the three golden balls were introduced to Britain around the fourteenth century when the Lombards from Northern Italy came

29

A good deed by St Nicholas may have given us the famous symbol of the pawnshop.

over as goldsmiths, bankers and moneylenders. They simply used this sign above their premises.

So why did the early pawnbrokers decide to erect balls? The first theory involves St Nicholas, alias Santa Klaus, Kris Kringle or Father Christmas, who was Bishop of Myra (now Mugla in Turkey) in Asia Minor in the fourth century. He is thought to have been born at Patara in Lycia. Amongst the many generous deeds attributed to him was one which involved saving three young women from a life of prostitution. Their father had been ruined financially and, heartbroken, he told them to leave home and fend for themselves. Nicholas heard about this, possibly even witnessing the banishment himself, and so quickly gave the girls a purse of gold coins each. This allowed the daughters return to their home and get the family back on their feet again. It is believed that pawnbrokers, as a tribute to St Nicholas (who is reputedly buried in Bari, southern Italy), and in an effort to associate themselves with helping the poor, adopted the three golden balls as their symbol.

Another theory revolves around the famed Medici family. The Medici had great power and wealth in the medieval period, giving the world two Popes (Leo X and Clement VII) and a queen of France (Catherine de Medici). They were also patrons of the arts (Lorenzo the Magnificent) and commerce (Cosimo de Medici). In financial circles, the name Medici was highly respected, a reputation pawnbrokers of the time yearned for. In an effort to draw some of that respect for themselves, it is believed that pawnbrokers looked at the coat of arms of the Medici, on which were numerous balls or pills (the word *medici* means 'physicians'), and imitated it. The three golden balls were meant to symbolise their expertise in financial matters like the celebrated Medici, and to show that they, the pawnbrokers, should be equally respected.

Three brass balls at Kearn's Pawnshop on Queen Street, near the Four Courts, in Dublin.

The circles on the Medici coat of arms, indeed, are themselves a matter of debate. Legend has it that a member of the Medici clan, Averdo, fighting for Charlemagne, slew a giant with either a three balled mace or with three sacks of rocks, and from this triumph came the Medici crest.

The fact that the House of Lombards, important moneylenders and pawnbrokers throughout Europe in the fourteenth century, used the three golden balls as the House's symbol, ensured that the sign would be associated with pawnshops far longer than even they might have expected.

Chapter Six

ON CANVAS, SCREEN AND PAGE

Money is better than poverty, if only for financial reasons.

Woody Allen (1935-)

Composers, writers and artists have for often drawn upon the image of pawnshops to inform, entertain or instill a conscience.

Pawnshops have appeared in numerous scenes in cinema and television productions, from Laurel and Hardy classics to *The Shawshank Redemption*. We see them in cartoons, and are mentioned regularly in dramas and soaps like *Coronation Street*. A hit song in the 1950s, sung by Guy Mitchell, was *Pittsburgh, Pennsylvania*, of which the opening verse goes:

> There's a pawnshop at the corner in Pittsburgh, Pennsylvania,
> And I walk up and down 'neath the clock,
> By the pawnshop on the corner in Pittsburgh, Pennsylvania,
> But I ain't got a thing left to hock ...

Charles Dickens presents a depressing image of a pawnshop in *Sketches by Boz*:

> Of all the numerous receptacles for misery and distress with which the streets of London unhappily abound, there are perhaps none which present such striking scenes of vice and poverty as the pawnbrokers shops.

William Hogarth, the eighteenth-century English artist, produced two fine prints in 1751 featuring dilapidated pawnshops. In these, titled *Gin Lane* and *Beer Street*, the names on the pawnshops are *S. Gripe* and *K. Pinch*, leaving us in no doubt as to the artist's opinion of pawnbrokers! In film, Charlie Chaplin's 1916 comedy, *The Pawnshop*, is in marked contrast with the serious and thought-provoking adaptation of Edward Lewis Wallant's novel, *The Pawnbroker*, made in 1964 and starring Rod Steiger. This latter story revolves around a Jewish pawnbroker, Sol Nazarman, who is haunted by his past in a Nazi Concentration Camp. One of the memorable lines from the novel reads: 'the shop creaked with the weight of other people's sorrows.'

Detail of 'Gin Lane' by William Hogarth, dating from 1751, showing the pawnshop as central to the artist's impression of low life in England.

Chaplin's silent movie, on the other hand, has the star clowning about inside and outside the pawnshop where he is employed. He catches a feather duster in an electric fan in one scene, breaks it and then carries out a medical examination of an alarm clock handed in as a

Charlie Chaplin on the set of his 1916 film, 'The Pawnshop'.

THE
PAWNBROKER
Edward Lewis Wallant

A rich and passionate book informed by real indignation at man's inhumanity to man . . . one to buy and read and think about THE LISTENER

Now filmed by the Landau Company starring ROD STEIGER Co-starring BROCK PETERS with Jaime Sanchez and GERALDINE FITZGERALD

3/6

The cover of the 1960s novel, The Pawnbroker.

pledge in another.

William Shakespeare mentions pawning in *Richard II*, as does Arthur Conan Doyle in *His Last Bow*. Anton Chekov refers to the pawning of scythes, caps and women's dresses by drunken men in his story *In the Ravine*. In Frodor Dostoyevsky's *Crime and Punishment*, the character Raskolnikov's pledging of his watch for one rouble and fifteen kopecks begins a tragic and murderous tale. On a lighter note, the nursery rhyme *Pop Goes the Weasel* means to pawn (pop) a particular shoemaking tool (weasel).

In Ireland, there have been numerous references to pawnshops, in our literature especially, but also on stage and film. Comedian Jimmy O'Dea had a recorded comic sketch set in a pawnshop, whilst the Alan Parker film, *The Commitments*, based on the Roddy Doyle book, features a musician trying out a set of drums in a pawnshop window. The Irish ballad *Solonika* has the lines: 'before I was married, I used to wear a shawl, but now that I'm married, the shawl is in the pawn.' Another old traditional Irish song *The Irish Rebellion* has the following lines:

Two by three they marched into the dining-room:
Young men, old men, girls who were not men at all;
Blind men, deaf men, men who had their teeth in pawn;

In J.P. Donleavy's *The Ginger Man*, two Waterford glass decanters are pawned for fifteen shillings near Dublin's Grafton Street ('Americans are mad for them').

Our more celebrated writers like James Joyce also used the

pawnshop in their stories, with Mrs White and Mrs McGuinness being pawnbrokers in *Ulysses*, where we read of:

> That awful drunkard of a wife of his. Setting up house for her time after time and then pawning the furniture on him every Saturday almost.

In *Dubliners*, the story 'Counterparts' gives more of an insight into pawning, where the main protagonist, Farrington, in desperate need of alcohol, pawns his watch for sixpence at Terry Kelly's pawnshop:

> He went through the narrow alley of Temple Bar quickly, muttering to himself that they could all go to hell because he was going to have a good night of it. The clerk in Terry Kelly's said *a crown*! but the consignor held out for six shillings; and in the end the six shillings was allowed him literally. He came out of the pawn-office joyfully, making a little cylinder of the coins between his thumb and fingers.

Peig Sayers, who lived on the Blasket Islands off County Kerry, told of Landlord Rice holding a cow in pawn. Padraic O' Conaire's story *Nell* centres around the life of a lonely pawnbroker, Nell Browne, whilst in Brendan Behan's *The Quare Fellow*, Dunlavin, a prisoner, speaks of the north city pawnshop. *Mary Makebelieve*, in James Stephens' *The Charwoman's Daughter*, has to rely on money from pawning during her illness.

In *Strumpet City*, James Plunkett tells of Pat Bannister, ready to pawn the shoes off his feet at Donegan's pawnshop:

> His immediate need was drink. He set off purposefully until he reached a shop with three brass balls hanging outside it.
> 'Are we doing business, Patrick?' Mr Donegan said pleasantly. He had been writing in his accounts book. Pat removed his jacket.
> 'This,' he said putting it on the counter.
> Mr Donegan adjusted his glasses and held it up to examine it.
> 'Your coat?' he questioned.

'How much?'

'How much do you want?'

'Half a crown.'

Mr Donegan made a clicking noise with his tongue. Pat was well known to him, a regular and reliable client. But he liked to make a business point.

'It's not worth half that.'

'Two shillings,' Pat compromised.

Mr Donegan wrote a docket and handed him half a crown.

'We'll leave it the half-crown.'

In 'The Drunkard', Frank O'Connor tells of a boy taken to a pub one day by his father on their way home from a funeral:

> I knew father was quite capable of lingering there til nightfall ... that next day father wouldn't go to work, and before the end of the week (mother) would be running down to the Pawn with the clock under her shawl.

In a more humorous vein, the Bard of Thomond, Michael Hogan, wrote a 109-verse poem about a court case in Cork in 1883 involving a Limerick pawnbroker and the woman he was engaged to, called *The Siege of the Golden Balls:*

You'll have your choice of costliest shawls,

Chains, brooches, gowns and overalls;

And you'll command my golden balls,

And polish them finely in Limerick.

Michael Hogan, the Bard of Thomond.

Not all references to pawnbroking in Ireland occur in fiction, however. In Gerry Adams' *Falls Memories*, and Paddy Crosbie's *Your Dinner's Poured Out* childhood experiences are shared, with both recalling the prominence of pawnshops in their respective localities of Belfast and Dublin.

These examples are only the tip of the iceberg. What, we might wonder, are our artistic or reflective contemporaries recalling or inventing for us? Visits to pawnshops have always made a deep impact on the more literary and learned element of society.

Chapter Seven

VISITORS VIEWS

Poverty keeps together more homes than it breaks up.

Saki (H.H. Munro) (1870-1916)

Visitors to Ireland have left us with many insights into the condition of Ireland and the Irish in previous centuries, and the trade of pawnbroking thankfully was not overlooked by these early travellers.

William Makepeace Thackeray, in 1842, whilst in Galway, told of a Captain Freeney pawning his watch. In Dublin, Thackeray remarked that the dandies wore hair pins:

> Large agate marbles or taws, globes terrestrial and celestial, pawn-brokers balls – I cannot find comparisons large enough for these wonderful ornaments of the person .

Henry D. Inglis, in 1834, when in Mallow wrote:

> I walked through the establishment of an extensive pawnbroker, and received from my visit no favourable impression of the condition of even those classes above that of the labouring poor. I saw numerous articles, the property of small farmers, articles worth from ten to thirty shillings, and generally pledged ... for payment of county rates. I was also told that at the time when tithes were sued for, the business of the establishment was extremely flourishing,

James O'Keeffe, a Carrick-on-Suir pawnbroker.

owing to the property in pawn by the farmers.

Later, Inglis noted:

> Pawnbrokers' shops are exceedingly numerous in all the towns; and
> by the common practice of pawning articles on Monday morning,
> and redeeming them on Saturday night, the interest on one shilling
> lent and received every week throughout the year, with the expense
> of the duplicate, amounts to 8s. 8d. per annum. The classes who deal
> with the pawnbrokers are not merely the lowest classes – labourers
> and artisans – but the small farmers also.

In 1866, when Philippe Daryl toured Ireland, he noted that the
rag and bone trade in Dublin was extremely active, and nearly
everyone was dressed in hand-me-downs: ' battered hats, dilapidated gowns, threadbare coats arrive here by the shiploads.'
Daryl pointed out that:

A pawnshop at Winetavern Street, Dublin, in the 1930s.

Now and then a pawnbroker with the three symbolic brass balls. [The pawnbroker] is a prominent figure in the daily drama of their wretched existence, the regulator of their humble exchequer through the coming and going of the necessaries of life, which they are obliged to part with periodically.

'You see that pair of hob-nailed shoes?' one of them tells me.

'For the last six months it has come here every Monday regularly and gone every Saturday. The possessor uses them only on Sundays; on weekdays he prefers enjoying his capital.'

His capital! – one shilling and sixpence, for which he has to pay an interest of one penny a week, ie, 300 per cent a year!

Usury, under all its forms, blooms spontaneously on that dung hill.

Daryl referred to the Charity Pawnshop in Limerick (see chapter eleven) and also gives us a valuable insight into the establishment known as the Money Office:

By the side of the pawnbroker a money office is almost always seen. It is an English institution ... upon the poor man's signature accompanied by those of two of his fellows, five and seven pounds

Cork's last pawnshop, William Jones of Shandon Street.

sterling will be lent to him, to be reimbursed by weekly instalments. But that resource, which is a powerful help for the strong energetic man, is almost invariably a cause of distress to the weak. The borrowed money ebbs out in worthless expenditure, in the buying of some articles of apparel or furniture, which soon takes the road to the pawnbroker's; and the debt alone remains weighing with all it's weight on poor Paddy. It is the last straw on the camel's back, and he ends by falling irremediably under it.

One would imagine from Daryl's remarks that people were literally dragged in off the streets and forced by pawnbrokers to pawn their goods. This is far from the truth. Unfortunate circumstances forced everyone from the lowest to the most revered to gladly approach the pawnbroker for loans.

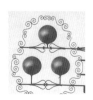

Chapter Eight

WHO PAWNED, AND WHAT DID THEY PAWN?

No man should commend poverty unless he is poor.

Saint Bernard (1091-1153)

It was not just the poor who pawned. The richest people on earth were happy to pledge their valuables to raise money for war or extravagant entertainment. It is known the Church was a good customer of pawnbrokers for many centuries (Pope John XXII's mitre was accepted in pawn by the Medici). So too were kings and royalty, who not infrequently pawned crowns and priceless gems. Charles the Bold, Duke of Burgundy; Guy, Count of Flanders; and Edward III were well known for their links with pawning. Queen Isabella of Spain pawned the crown jewels to finance the voyage to America of Christopher Columbus.

Pawnbrokers over a period of time, in different continents and cultures, dealt with people who went on to become high income earners – doctors, lawyers, even television celebrities. The majority of the clientele were, however, the ordinary working people who would consider comfort as not having to pawn for a week or two. *Shawlies* were very familiar inside the doors of pawnshops. Most of the customers were living in the traditional labouring areas like council estates or flats or down laneways and alleyways, places invariably with higher unemployment than the more affluent locations. Oftentimes, ironically, people in these communities had actually more disposable income than the perceived 'better off ' in the exclusive enclaves. High income earners, irrespective of address, frequently pawned because they may have squandered their money on a drinking habit or in betting shops. Regarding gender, it seems women were more likely to be seen in pawnshops than were men. This

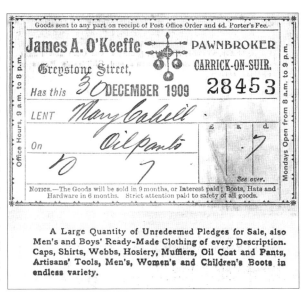

Front and back of a 1909 pawn ticket from James O'Keeffe's pawnshop in Carrick-on-Suir.

could have been because men felt it a slight on their characters that they had to resort to pawnshops. Alcoholics and children were not supposed to pawn, but these were often served by clerks. To attract customers, pawnbrokers advertised like any other business – through newspapers, sandwich boards, leaflets and word of mouth: 'Liberal advances on everything of value', 'Any amount to lend', and 'Unlimited cash advance' they boasted, or the emphasis might be more on discretion: 'Most privately situated pawn office', 'Very, very private and convenient'. Another method was to boast of the quality: 'First class pawn office', or the angle might be: 'Extensive storage', or 'Speed', which may have been aimed at self-conscious people anxious to get in and out of the pawnshop before being seen.

Anything and everything ended up in pawnshops. Desperate for money, people would bring whatever they could lay their hands on. In January 1830, Rev. Sheehan of Rathcormac in County Cork wrote to the *Cork Constitution* newspaper requesting:

'should blankets stamped in the corner with the words Rathcormac Charity be offered to persons in the pawnbroking business, they be detained.'

In the same month in Cork city, Jeremiah Mahony and Patrick Flynn were given six months imprisonment and 'moderate whipping' for stealing a cloak and giving it to a woman named Catherine Mahony to pawn for them at Mrs Hare's pawnshop.

For the pawnbroker, even the most ridiculous pledge would be accepted if he knew his customer, and was satisfied that he would return to redeem the pledge. After all, the whole purpose was to make a profit, so whether it be gold or garbage, once there was money to be made that was fine by the pawnbroker. He would have to be more careful with someone he did not know, or knew to be unreliable. The last thing the pawnbroker wanted was to be left with a pledge that no one would buy from him at auction. At any given time in history, the nature of the pledges was a good indication of household or work implements, or of clothing in vogue. Tradesmen, like coopers, pawned their specialised tools. Wives pawned cutlery or anything else at hand in the home. Even known prostitutes in Dublin and elsewhere stole watches and

Some racing pigeon clocks – one of the many types of goods still pledged.

1 _____ Gold Dress Ring	47 _____ Gold Clown & Gold Chain
2 _____ Gold Earrings	48 _____ Gents Gold Ring
3 _____ 2 Gold Rings	49 _____ 2 Gents Gold Rings
4 _____ Metal Core Bangle	50 _____ Gents Gold Signet Ring
5 _____ Gold Dress Ring	51 _____ 2 Gold Chains
6 _____ Gold Hoop Earrings	52 _____ 2 Gold Rings
7 _____ Gold Chain & Gold Bracelet	53 _____ Gold Chain & Gold Bracelet
8 _____ Gold Horse Head Ring	54 _____ 2 Gold Rings
9 _____ Gents Gold College Ring	55 _____ Gold Ring & Gold Bracelet
10 _____ Gold Fob & Gold Chain	56 _____ Gold 3 Stone Diamond Ring
11 _____ 2 Gents Gold Rings	57 _____ 2 Gold Rings
12 _____ St George Gold Ring	58 _____ 2 Gents Gold Rings
13 _____ Gold Ring & Gold Bracelet	59 _____ 3 Gold Rings
14 _____ Gold Ring	60 _____ 2 Gold Rings
15 _____ St George Gold Pendant & Gold Chain	61 _____ Gold Clown Ring
16 _____ 2 Gents Gold Rings	62 _____ 2 Gold Necklets
17 _____ Gold Ring & Gold Bracelet	63 _____ 3 Gold Rings
18 _____ Gold Dress Ring	64 _____ Gold Gate Bracelet
19 _____ 2 Gold Rings	65 _____ 3 Gold Rings
20 _____ Gents Gold College Ring	66 _____ 3 Gold Chains
21 _____ 18ct Single Stone Diamond Ring	67 _____ Gold Cluster Diamond Ring
22 _____ Gold Pendant & Gold Chain	68 _____ 3 Gold Rings & Gold Chain
23 _____ Gold 2 Stone Diamond Ring	69 _____ 3 Gold Rings
24 _____ 2 Gold Rings	70 _____ 18ct Diamond & Sapphire Ring
25 _____ Gold Pendant & Gold Chain	71 _____ 18ct Single Stone Diamond Ring
26 _____ Gold Half Soverign Ring	72 _____ Gents Gold College Ring
27 _____ Gold Clown & Gold Chain	73 _____ 2 Gold Rings
28 _____ 3 Gold Rings	74 _____ 2 Gold Rings
29 _____ Gold Ring & Gold Chain	75 _____ Gold Pendant & Gold Chain
30 _____ 18ct Figaro Chain	76 _____ Gents Gold College Ring
31 _____ Gold Horse & Gold Chain	77 _____ 2 Gents Gold Rings
32 _____ 18ct Diamond Ring	78 _____ 3 Gents Gold Rings
33 _____ 2 Gold Bangles	79 _____ Gents Gold Onyx Ring
34 _____ 2 Pairs Gold Earrings & Gold Bracelet	80 _____ Gold Cross & Gold Chain
35 _____ 3 Gold Rings	81 _____ Gents Gold Onyx Ring
36 _____ Gold Bangle & Gold Pendant	82 _____ 2 Gold Necklets
37 _____ 2 Gents Gold Rings	83 _____ Gold Clown & Gold Chain
38 _____ 2 Gents Gold Rings	84 _____ 2 Gold Rings
39 _____ Gents Gold Horse Head Ring	85 _____ Gold Gate Bracelet
40 _____ Gents Gold Bracelet	86 _____ 2 Gold Rings
41 _____ Gold Mum Ring	87 _____ Gold Ring & Gold Necklet
42 _____ Gold Dad Ring	88 _____ Gold Gate Bracelet
43 _____ 2 Gents Gold Rings	89 _____ Stamp Collection
44 _____ 2 Ladies Gold Rings	90 _____ 3 Figureens
45 _____ Gold T-Bar Chain	91 _____ 2 Gold Rings
46 _____ Gold Locket & Gold Chain	92 _____ 3 Gents Gold Rings

Extract from list of pawned goods sold at auction.

valuables from their customers and pawned them nearby. The following are examples of the pledges in Ireland down the years:

Artificial limbs, boxing gloves, bird cages, barrel organs, bicycles, books, bricks, carriages, clothing, crutches, dolls, elephant tusks, false teeth, guns, hearing aids, jewellery, lavatory bowls, medals, money, pension books, pigeon clocks, razors, records, skeletons, statues, tools, ventriloquist dolls, xylophones (candidate for the 1859 elections in Galway redeemed a local band's instruments from a pawnshop, no doubt expecting support in return).

Men's suits were amongst the most popular of pawns, more so than women's clothes which went out of fashion quicker and thus fetched less from the pawnbroker. A shine on a pants or coat or any threadbare appearance devalued them, so many people kept everyday clothes literally for use everyday, and then very carefully they kept aside the best of clothing, which was strictly used for pawning. Many men were too proud to be seen inside a pawnshop or to have their wife pawn, but the women went to all sorts of trouble to hide the fact that the next meal was a result of an item of clothing being 'at the Uncle's'. The sad fact is that many men spent their wages on alcohol, and wives had to pawn because of their husband's selfishness. Pride was not a luxury the woman could afford. Despite well-laid plans, an unexpected mid-week funeral or function would expose the fact that the husband's best suit was in pawn, and the wife would often have to pay with more than just a verbal bashing for humiliating her spouse.

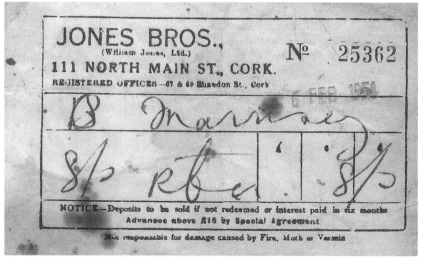

A pawntickets from 1954 – note 'not responsible for damage caused by fire, moths or vermin'.

Once pledges were landed on the shelves of pawnshops, their safe keeping was not totally guaranteed. Because of the absence of central heating in all shops long ago, staff were glad to light open fires on the premises. This presented a hazard in itself. It was not unknown for a pawnshop to be burned to the ground, with all the pledges inside. This happened to William Delaney's shop at Broad Street, Limerick on 9 January 1860. One can only imagine the despair and plight of the people who had pledged their only goods of value. Fire was not the only hazard. There was no guarantee either given by some pawnbrokers against an attack by moth or vermin on articles pawned.

Whatever was pledged, it was, more often than not, a treasured possession, and many a tear was shed when the owner could not redeem his or her ornament, ring or item of clothing. Sometimes people were so desperate that they were forced to obtain money by selling their pawn ticket to a third party, thus losing their pledge forever.

Pawning was a fact of life for people, something as regular in their lives as going to a match or a Sunday stroll. Most people took any indignity or inconvenience brought upon by a visit to a pawnshop in their stride, and later looked back with much gratitude for the assistance given by the pawnbroker in their bleakest hours of need.

And so now we know who pawned, but who were the pawnbrokers ?

Chapter Nine

WHO WERE THE PAWNBROKERS?

That's another advantage of being poor – a doctor will cure you faster.
Kin (F. McKinney) Hubbard (1868-1930)

Who were the pawnbrokers of Ireland, where were they based, and just what was the attraction of opening a pawnshop? One step inside the doorway of an average pawnshop might surely have been enough to raise most people's eyebrows. Crowds of noisy customers shouting each other down, shoving and pushing, pungent smells stagnating the air, clerks rushing to and fro screaming names and figures, with one hand pulling sand-covered pawn tickets from a drawer, with the other scribbling down details of the next pledge. And on top of this there was the bother from drunks and the threat of robbery. In a two-day period in 1825, Cork Assizes convicted a woman, Catherine Rice, for stealing a nineteen-yard length of material from a pawnshop: Rice received seven years transportation for her crime. Another woman, Bridget Symmons, stole clothing from a pawnbroker in the same city and was given three months' imprisonment. But the one thing which compensated the pawnbrokers for all of these difficult conditions was the high expectancy of profit.

The promise of making a good living from pawnbroking persuaded enough people who had amassed sufficient money to take the plunge and open shop. Not everyone succeeded, yet many

Quirke's pawnshop (right of picture), Nenagh, County Tipperary, in the 1890s.

were willing to opt out of respectable jobs like teaching to open pawnshops. In Cork in the 1890s, Mr P.H. Meade, who owned three pawnshops and other property in the city, was the son of a cooper. Coopering was a well paid and enviable trade at that time, and few, other than sons of coopers themselves, were allowed an apprenticeship. Therefore to turn down this opportunity in favour of pawnbroking seems to have been a risk Meade felt worth taking, and one that by all accounts proved beneficial. No academic qualifications were required to be a pawnbroker. All one needed was money, some people to vouch for you, and for a few friends or associates to put up bonds (although the latter two clauses were regularly not adhered to).

Pawnbrokers were, in general, ordinary people, out to make a pretty ordinary living. Most did just that, quietly and without causing their customers or the authorities difficulties.

Little is known about the identity of pawnbrokers in Ireland before the nineteenth century, but a few names are thankfully recorded, such as Alexander Blood and William Perry, who both lodged bonds to enter the trade in Limerick city in 1791. William Hughes of Drogheda followed suit in 1795, with James Hunter accompanying him in the same town in 1796. We also know that one of the founding members of the renowned Dublin charity, The Sick and Indigent Roomkeepers Society, established at Mountrath Street in 1790, was a pawnbroker, Timothy Nowlan of 14 Greek Street. Soon after contemporary trade directories filled with pawnbrokers names in increasing numbers. In 1788, there were 51 pawnbrokers in Ireland, 49 of these in Dublin, one in Cork and one in Waterford, five of which ceased trading within the year.

In 1800, there was still just one pawnshop in Cork. Belfast had three in 1810, but by 1824, over 200 pawnbrokers traded in the island. The largest concentration was, as one would expect, in the larger cities. Dublin had 46 pawnshops, Cork 35, with Belfast and Waterford 23 each. On a provincial basis, Munster had 109 pawnshops, Leinster 56, Ulster 40 and Connacht four (all in Galway). Outside these cities, statistics reveal that thirteen pawnshops were open in Limerick, followed by Bandon and Newry with six

each. On average, there was one pawnshop catering for 10,000 people in Ireland in 1824, but there were quite a few notable exceptions. Although there were over 13,000 people in Sligo, there is no record of a pawnshop trading there at that time. At the other end of the scale, Bandon had no less than six for 12,000 people, Clonmel five for 16,000, Newry six for 13,500 , and Lisburn three for 4,500 people.

Undoubtedly, these pawnshops did not just cater for the towns in question

Grehan's Pawnshop, Naas, County Kildare.

alone and would have had customers from rural communities. Nonetheless, it is clear that the strength of the trade differed from town to town. By 1835 there were 50 in Cork and 41 in Belfast. Around this time, pawnbrokers were prominent in political movements, such as the backing of the radical People's Hall in Cork, and also a decade later in the same city the anti-Minister's Money campaign (Minister's Money was a levy on property in the bigger towns and cities for the upkeep of Protestant clergy). Pawnbrokers were associated with the Liberal Club in County Carlow. A Youghal witness to the *Poor Law Enquiry* in 1835 stated that through contacts with the 'lowest class', pawnbrokers were able to take political advantage. Much later, in 1868, a Protestant pawnbroker, during elections in Dublin, changed his party allegiance and took with him enough details on prominent figures many of whom were heavily in debt to cause considerable unease. Earlier still, in 1837, there were 445 pawnbrokers making Returns to the Marshal of Dublin. Michael (or Maurice) Nowlan issued the most pledges that year in the country, with 127,598 tickets, but it was Henry Booth of the same city, who lent a higher amount – £31,301 in respect of 106,592 pawn tickets, as against Nowlan lending £15,220. This suggests that Booth accepted higher value pledges than Nowlan – Booth might have taken in more jewellery, whilst Nowlan may have accepted more low value items like clothing. Around this time, it must be noted there was thought to be a few hundred unregistered pawnbrokers trading in Ireland, as well as those legally trading.

After the Great Famine, the trade began to pick up again. In 1856, there were over 500 pawnshops countrywide. Belfast (62), Dublin (48) and Cork (42) again led the way, but a wider spread is in evidence around the provinces. Munster had 195 pawnshops Leinster and Ulster 130 each, and Connacht 31. In these figures, Limerick took a share of 22, Waterford eleven, Derry and Newry ten each, Clonmel nine, Galway, Drogheda and Armagh eight each, Carlow and Youghal seven a piece, and six in Dungarvan. In England, by comparison, outside London, Manchester had 170,

Liverpool 121, Birmingham 96, Bristol 33, Leeds 29 and Sheffield with 23.

In 1867 there were over 600 pawnshops in Ireland, with more than 3,500,000 million pawn tickets being issued in one year in Dublin alone. There were 53 pawnshops trading in Dublin (compared to about 600 in London). In 1881, Belfast, with over 100, exceeded the total number trading in the capital. Dublin had 46 whilst Cork had now only 28. On a provincial basis, Ulster dominated the trade with some 200 pawnshops, Leinster had 149, Munster with 139 and Connacht with 31. In all, more than 500 pawnshops were now trading on the island of Ireland, a massive increase from 100 years earlier. What is noticeable is the far wider spread of locations. Most of the bigger towns now had at least one pawnbroker. Sligo, with five, had one more pawnshop than Galway. Tuam and Westport had three each in the same province

A pawnshop in Athlone, c. 1900.

of Connacht. Clonmel, with ten pawnshops, only trailed behind Cork, Limerick (twenty) and Waterford (thirteen) in Munster, with Dungarvan (six) and Carrick-on-Suir (five) not far behind. In Ulster, Derry followed Belfast with eleven, then Newry with eight, and Armagh and Ballymena with five each. Finally in Leinster, apart from Dublin, Drogheda had six, and then four towns had five each – Kilkenny, Kingstown, Athlone and Dundalk.

In 1893, the figure of licensed pawnbrokers in

the country had dropped to 420. Of these, Belfast was still way ahead with 100 pawnbrokers, Dublin city next with 50, Cork city with 23, Limerick city with fifteen, then Derry and Kilkenny with ten each. It is interesting to note that in that same year, over 11,500,000 pawn tickets were issued in Ireland, and £1,603,786 lent by pawnbrokers.

Pawnshops were as common on the Main Street of towns such as Thurles, Templemore and Cashel in County Tipperary, Loughrea in Galway, Castlebar in County Mayo, and in Cavan town, as well as in the alleys and back streets of cities and other towns up and down the country. They could be large and imposing shops, taking up sizeable sections of a street, or they could be small and unassuming. On the one hand premises such as Ellen O'Donovan's pawnshop in Sligo town in 1870 could be sandwiched between two pubs, whilst Hugh Scott in Belfast had no fewer than three premises almost adjacent at numbers 117, 119 and 203 on the Shankill Road.

Most pawnshops were registered in the name of men, but a not insignificant proportion had women as licencees. In 1844, for example, of the 467 legally licensed pawnbrokers in the country, 54 were women, and the longest-trading pawnbroker in the island at the time was in fact a female, Mary Hosford of Cork, who had taken out a licence 32 years earlier.

Pawnbrokers were people who accumulated a bit of money or maybe inherited the business from their parents. Their names – Dohertys, Murphys, McKees, Chillingworths, Trowsdales – reflect the different denominations

Pat Kearns, a present-day pawnbroker at Queen Street, Dublin.

Carthy's pawnshop, near the Pro Cathedral, Dublin.

and hues of Irish society.

When registering, pawnbrokers asked people from all walks of life to act as their sureties – attorneys, brewers, coopers, doctors, farmers, grocers, ironmongers, hotel keepers, jewellers, publicans, silversmiths, tanners, surgeons and teachers, to name but a few. Established pawnbrokers themselves acted as sureties, often more than once. Samuel Smith of Henry Street in Dublin was surety for no less than eight other pawnbrokers at the one time. Some combined pawnbroking with other activities. In Cork in 1824, George Divett was both a quilt dealer and a pawnbroker, whilst in Armagh, at the same time, John Ross traded as a rag merchant cum pawnbroker. In 1870, Patrick O'Flanagan of Durrow was a draper, whilst in Moate, County Westmeath, Thomas Glanville was a grocer, baker and postmaster. Ulick Walsh, pawnbroker, also sold leather in Carrick-on-Shannon; whilst at Rathfryland, County Down, David Todd also traded as a butter and provision merchant. Other people down the years combined the business of accepting pawns with trades such as auctioneering, or stamp distribution, ironmongery or, in one case, in Doneraile in County Cork, where William Foley was also a 'Master Extraordinary in Chancery and Commissioner for taking Affadavits'.

The religious beliefs of those involved in pawnbroking would have been predominately Christian – Protestant at first more than likely, due to the trading restrictions placed on Catholics from the Penal Laws, and then in due course, Catholic, with only a handful at any given time being of a different religion.

It is interesting to note that whilst pawnbrokers were free to attend their services, the Irish Methodist Community forbade pawnbrokers from holding an office in the church, as the pawnbrokers were not considered friends of the poor, i.e., they took advantage of their plight.

One Dublin pawnbroker contributed to a fund to help Pope Pius IX out of difficulties arising from an Italian unification campaign.

Of the 64 pawnbrokers in County Cork in 1875, 32 were Catholic, 24 Protestant Episcopalian, seven Methodist, and one other unrecorded denomination – perhaps Jewish?

In common lore, the Jewish community has been associated with the trade, but in reality, in this country at least, they were poorly represented in it. In fact, there cannot have been many Jews trading as pawnbrokers, and this is down to simple arithmetic – there were never that many Jewish people residing in Ireland at any one time, not enough to figure strongly in such a geographically widespread trade.

Whatever the religious persuasion, whatever the background, whatever the address, all pawnbrokers were linked by one crucial obligation – to abide by very specific laws.

Chapter Ten

RULES ARE RULES

To be poor and independent is very nearly an impossibility.

William Cobbett (1762-1835)

Until 1964, the pawnbroking trade, for the most part, had to comply with legislation going back nearly 200 years. Up to early 1786, the laws aimed at eliminating usury made it very difficult for pawnbrokers in Ireland to ply their trade legally. It was unlawful to charge more than six per cent per annum on any size loan, no matter the amount or trouble and expense faced by pawnbrokers in so doing. Thus pawnbrokers either issued bigger loans or illegally charged higher interest than the six per cent allowable. On 1 May, 1786, during the reign of King George III, this was all to change. On that date, the first known laws in relation to commercial pawnbroking in Ireland came into effect. The man behind the move to bring pawning under some semblance of control was the M.P. for Banagher, Peter Holmes.

What, then, were the new laws aimed at allowing pawnbrokers more scope in relation to the charging of interest, and perhaps more importantly, meant to tackle the widespread abuses prevalent at that time?

Firstly, only people 'of good and honest repute' could henceforth open a pawnshop. No one owning a public house or selling alcohol could obtain a licence. The would-be pawnbroker was obliged to lodge a bond of £300 himself to the local town clerk, plus three separate bonds of £100 each from three other 'respectable people'. After the town clerk processed the application (for which he received a fee of six shillings and eight pence), a certificate was to be forwarded to the Marshal of the City of Dublin. The Marshal was to register the application, obtain five shillings for his troubles, and then ensure that the new pawnbroker would send him, from then on, monthly Returns of all his income and expenditure, with a fee of one shilling per Return. The details were then to be sent by the Marshal to Parliament. The new pawnbroker was obliged to paint above the shop his name and the word 'Pawnbroker(s)', in

King George III, who was on the throne when the Irish laws on pawnshops were introduced in 1786. Painting by John Zoffany.

lettering of at least four inches long, before he commenced trading.

Pawnbrokers main source of income was from loan interest charged, and also from the issuing of tickets, called duplicates, for which he received a fee on issue to a customer. The legislation regulated the amounts he could charge in each instance. The interest chargeable depended on the size of the loan. For instance, on a loan of one shilling and eight pence, he could only charge a halfpenny per month, whilst for a bigger loan of £10, he was to charge four shillings and two pence per month.

The tickets themselves had to conform to clauses in the new Act. They had to be made of fairly strong paper, be able to take writing, have enough room to write all relevant details, viz. names of pawner and pawnbroker, full description of goods pawned, and the amount of the loan. The onus was on the person pawning to keep this ticket in a safe place. When it came to redeeming the item

AT

KEARNS'S MONEY OFFICE

69 QUEEN STREET

You can obtain, Without Delay

HIGHEST CASH ADVANCES

On MOTOR BIKES, PIANOS, FURNITURE, JEWELLERY,
CAMERAS, SEWING MACHINES, WEARING APPAREL, Etc., Etc.

Special Private Entrance for Motors,
Furniture, Etc., at Oxmantown Place.

Superior and Extensive Ware-rooms for High-class Articles.

Is most privately situated, within five minutes from O'Connell
Bridge and Park Gate.

Near the tram line, but not on it

Near the tram line, but not on it

Advertisement for Kearns Money Office.

pawned, the pawnbroker could not be held accountable if it transpired that someone other than the owner produced the duplicate at the counter and the pawnbroker innocently handed him back the pledge once appropriate money exchanged hands. If the owner of a pawn ticket reported his pawn ticket lost or destroyed, he could make an affidavit to the justice of the peace and then redeem his goods at the pawnshop.

Not surprisingly, the pawnbroker was obliged under the Act to keep full details of all his transactions in his books.

One of the main advantages to customers has always been the fact that pawnbrokers have to retain the items pledged for some time before the goods could be sold on. This gives and gave people a chance to gather money together and reclaim their property. In the 1786 legislation the period for which the goods had to be kept (in as good a condition as they came in) depended on the size of the loan. For loans up to twenty shillings, the pawnbroker could not send the goods to auction before six months had expired. On loans of between twenty and 40 shillings, the retention time was nine months, whilst it increased to twelve months for loans above that. If the customer came in at any time to pay the due interest, the pawnbroker had to retain the goods for a further period of time, again depending on the amount of the loan.

The auctioning of unredeemed pawns was also very central to the trade of pawnbroking. Pawnbrokers' auctioneers themselves were to be of a high calibre, and they too had to lodge the same amount in bonds as the pawnbrokers. The Act ordered that certain procedures must be followed to ensure the customers interests were protected. The pawnbroker, at the expiry of the term for which he had to retain unredeemed goods, was to get the goods valued by an appraiser. The appraiser had to record his valuation and give copies to the pawnbroker. The pawnbroker was to contact the person who pawned the goods advising him when and where his property was going to be auctioned, if he, the pawner, did not redeem the goods within fourteen days of this notification. If he could not contact his customer, the pawnbroker was to put up posters at the nearest market or court house, announcing details of the auction. If the customer still did not redeem his goods, they were to be sold to the highest bidder at auction. If they were sold at auction for more than the loan initially given to the person pawning the difference (known as the overplus) was to be given back to the owner, less auctioning costs. The auctioneer had to keep a record of the sale, so that the person pawning could inspect the details at any time to ensure he was not being cheated. There was a cost of one penny for each inspection. The same entitlement (and fee) applied to the inspection of pawnbrokers' records.

As the pawning of stolen goods was an ongoing problem, the 1786 Act directed that anyone found guilty of this offence would be fined twenty shillings or, if he was unable to pay, be sent to prison for fourteen days hard labour. If by the eleventh day in prison, he had not arranged to have the money repaid, he would be whipped. Any surplus from the twenty shillings fine was to go to the poor, via the local Protestant minister or church warden. The pawnbroker, too, was liable for punishment if he knowingly accepted stolen goods. He would be fined double the amount of the loan, as well as returning the stolen goods to the rightful owner. The authorities were entitled to search a pawnshop for stolen goods at any time, and if a pawnbroker hindered or refused entrance, he would be fined £5 or sent to five days hard labour in prison.

Other offences included operating a pawnshop without a licence (a fine of between £10 and £20 per offence, or a term of prison with hard labour of between three and six months), refusing to pay an overplus to a customer (a fine of treble the amount of the loan), selling alcohol in tandem with operating a pawnshop (a ten pound fine), refusing to allow the inspection of books (a five pound punishment), selling pawned goods outside the manner allowed by law (a five pound fine), damaging goods while in pawn (the customer was to be fully compensated), failing to have proper details on pawn tickets (40 shillings to be forfeited), failure to make monthly returns to the Marshal of Dublin (another 40 shillings), failure to replace deceased sureties (a fine of £5).

Disputes between pawnbrokers and their customers were to be settled by the Justice of Peace. Normally, those in dispute had to take oaths, but if either were Quakers, a solemn affirmation was sufficient. This 1786 Act was to prove the cornerstone of legislation governing pawnbroking for almost two centuries, though important revisions and additions were made within two years of the enactment.

THE 1788 ACT

In 1788 an Act was introduced 'to explain, amend and render more effectual' the initial Act of two years earlier. Much of the new laws pertained to Dublin only, yet some important changes involved the whole 32 counties of Ireland. New rates of loan interest came into effect. For example, the pawnbroker could charge a halfpenny per month on a loan of between one shilling and less than two shillings, and the scale went up according to the size of the loan. A two-pound loan would cost ten pence interest per month. These charges included the cost incurred by the pawnbroker in warehousing. The pawnbroker was ordered not to divide up a loan to his customers, as this practice had allowed pawnbrokers charge for several duplicate tickets instead of just the one. One loan, one ticket was the new instruction. Any offence meant a twenty-shillings fine.

For the first time, opening hours of pawnshops were to be regulated. From now on pawnshops could not open on Sundays. Furthermore, they were allowed to open only during certain hours of the rest of the week. This depended on the season. From 25 March to 29 September, trading was between 10am and 7pm. For the rest of the year, closing time was back to 4pm. A 40-shilling fine ensued for any offence on this matter.

The issue of stolen goods was again targeted in the 1788 Act. Because altering or removing identifiable marks from silverware and such valuables was making it difficult for the police to trace stolen goods, pawnbrokers were warned that criminal offences would be brought against them if they accepted such items. Fines for unregistered pawnbrokers were now increased by £5 per offence from the fines in the earlier Act.

Where Dublin pawnshops were concerned (those within a three-mile radius of the city), the 1788 Act brought about some interesting rules specifically for the trade in the capital.

One was that pawnbrokers had to put up securities of £1,000 each, plus three other bonds of £300 each, far larger than their colleagues in the rest of Ireland. These high bonds went to pay for the police force in Dublin. A similar idea, incidentally, was considered at the Court of D'Oyer Hundred in Cork in 1828, when Sheriff Savage put forward the notion of pawnbrokers paying £100 each for a licence to establish a local police force of twelve men, a suggestion repeated in 1830 at a general meeting aimed at establishing a Watch for Cork in 1830.

Pawnbrokers in Dublin had to get character references from the police, a church warden and five other respectable people. Disputes between Dublin pawnbrokers and their customers had to be settled either by Magistrate, Justice of Peace, the police or the Court of Quarter Sessions, depending on the amount in dispute. Dublin pawnbrokers found to have knowingly handled stolen goods faced having their pawnbroking licences withdrawn. Further offences were the selling of pawned goods without notifying the customer of the auction, or by holding the said auction outside one of the four approved Divisional Auction Rooms in Dublin – Capel Street, Wood Quay, Church Street and Merchants Quay. This breach of law resulted in a five-pound fine.

Regarding auctions, special new regulations were introduced for the capital city. Up until 1788, the Sword Bearer and the Marshal both received fees for appraising articles pawned in the area, fees which were now terminated. The Sword Bearer and Marshal, however, were allowed to continue as pawnbrokers auctioneers, with the help of two further people. Thus there were now four pawnbrokers' auctioneers in Dublin, one per Divisional Ward – Stephen's Green, Rotunda, Workhouse and Barrack Wards (these being the old police divisions). Each Divisional auctioneer was ordered to have proper and spacious rooms as near as possible to the centre of his ward. He could not hold auctions of forfeited pledges outside his own ward, or he would be fined £10 if caught doing so. The auctioneers had to pay the same bonds as Dublin pawnbrokers and take an oath before the police. Their fees for auctioneering were a penny per shilling for any article they sold for less than twenty shillings, a shilling and four pence for amounts of between twenty and 40 shillings, and a shilling per one pound for amounts over 40 shillings. These fees were instead of any costs for warehousing, room rent, advertising, postage, and payment of staff.

A few other portions of the 1788 Act are also worth noting. For goods fetching no more than loans of four shillings, pawnbrokers did not have to serve notices of auction. Loans of more than four shillings required the Registers in Dublin to issue detailed notices of auction to the pawnbroker's customers, these to be issued within six days of being notified to do so by the pawnbroker. If the Register (who received fees of three to four pence per notice) failed to issue notices of auction to the pawnbrokers customers, he became liable for any loss suffered by the pawnbroker or his customer. The Register had to keep records of his notices, much like each auctioneer and pawnbroker.

MISCELLANEOUS ACTS

The 1788 Act was to be the last major legislation covering the pawnbroking trade in Ireland until the second half of the twentieth century, but there were some small amendments in the intervening year. These included provisions to send lawbreaking pawnbrokers to the House of Correction in the Dublin *Magistrate's Act* of 1808, laws relating to Charitable Loan Societies in 1823, 1829, 1836, 1842 and 1843, a law ordering a reduction in stamp duty payable by Dublin pawnbrokers (to £7 10 shillings) in 1854, the prohibiting of accepting firearms or ammunitions as pawns in the *Firearms Act* of 1925, the order to pawnbrokers not to serve drunks in 1908 legislation, and the *Children's Act* of 1908 also, wherein it was deemed an offence for a pawnbroker to accept pawns from under fourteens (see Bibliography for a detailed list of the relevant Acts). Further laws which effected the pawnbroking trade ranged from the *Pension Books Act* of 1932, which prohibited anyone accepting pension books or related documents in pawn, the *Shops Acts* of 1938, which spelt out rights for employees of retailers and obligatory closure of pawnshops for a half day per week, to the *Pawnbrokers Divisional Auctioneers Act* of 1943, which permitted the four divisional auctioneers in Dublin to hold their auctions outside their own respective division if they so desired.

New laws on pawnbroking in Ireland were proposed by the Attorney General, Mr Smith, and a Mr Hamilton in a Bill in 1843, which intended considerable amendments to help the better running of the trade and bring it more in line with it's

Sign on display at Breretons Pawnshop, Capel Street, Dublin.

English counterpart, but their efforts failed.

THE 1964 ACT

The year 1964 saw the next major law change for pawnbroking in Ireland (which, it should be remembered, now excluded the six counties of Northern Ireland, whereas the 1786 and 1788 Acts covered the whole island).

The *Pawnbroker's Act* of 1964 was brought in by future Taoiseach, Charles J. Haughey, who was then Minister for Justice. The legislation applied to every pawn for which an advance not exceeding £50 was made by a pawnbroker (or one of his staff) to the customer. The licensing procedure for becoming a pawnbroker involved the applicant contacting the District Court for a certificate authorising the grant to him of a licence. The applicant forwarded this certificate to the Revenue Commissioners, plus any excise duty payable, and the Commissioners then endorsed the application. An application could be refused for a number of reasons: poor character of the applicant or no financial stability; if he held a bookmaker's, intoxicating liquor or auctioneer's licence. Appeals against such a judgement could be lodged with the Circuit Court. The Revenue Commissioners could issue temporary, seven-day licences in these situations. Pawnbrokers licences could be suspended or withdrawn if the pawnbroker was convicted of larceny, knowingly received stolen goods, fraud or if he broke conditions laid down by the Act.

The pawnbroker had to display, in large and legible characters, his name and the word 'Pawnbroker' above the door of his shop. Inside, he was obliged to place in a prominent position for his customers a notice showing the following: a halfpenny loan interest for every two shillings lent, a two-penny charge for every pawn ticket issued, two pence valuation fee on each five shillings lent, sixpence for every inspection of a sale book or auctioneer's catalogue, and sixpence for a form of declaration. The notice was also to state that pledges (other than gold or precious metals and stones) must be redeemed within six months and seven days; if interest was, however, paid over by the pawner in that time, the six months and seven days limit would start again. For gold and other precious items, this period was one year and seven days.

For loans of £2 or under, the pawnbroker was allowed to keep the goods if they were not redeemed in the given time. Regarding loans over £2, the goods had to be sent to public auction. Any overplus received from the sale could be reclaimed by the pawner within the following twelve months. The pawner could inspect the pawnbroker's books or auctioneer's catalogue within that time, paying a fee of sixpence for the privilege of inspection.

If a pledge was damaged by fire whilst in the pawnbroker's possession, the pawner was entitled to receive back half the amount of the loan. If the pledge was damaged through wilful neglect of the pawnbroker, the pawner could seek compensation through the District Court. If a pawner lost his pawn ticket, he was to immediately tell the pawnbroker, who would give him a form of declaration. The pawner was to bring this to a Peace Commissioner or Commissioner for Oaths. If the pawn ticket was not reported lost, the pawnbroker was obliged to hand over the pledge to anyone who produced the ticket at the counter. On pawn tickets, the pawnbroker was obliged to give a pawn ticket to his customer, who must take it. 'Special Contract Pawn Tickets' could be issued by the pawnbroker in respect of loans more than £10. The pawnbroker had to keep proper sale and pledge books. He had to give loans in current, legal money. He was forbidden to divide up loans into smaller sums, accept pawns from under sixteens, employ under sixteens to take in pledges, accept pawns from known drunks or those intoxicated before him, accept pawn tickets issued by other pawnbrokers, purchase (except at public auction) any pledge in pawn with him, accept any firearms or ammunition in pawn. The pawnbroker was not bound to hand over a pledge unless the pawn ticket was produced by the customer. It was an offence for anyone to give false information about ownership of an item he offered as a pawn, or to refuse to explain how it came into his possession, or attempt to redeem goods without being entitled to do so.

Every auction of pawnbrokers' pledges was to be conducted by a ministerially-appointed auctioneer. The pawnbroker had the right to bid for pledges pawned with him. The Gardai were obliged to notify pawnbrokers of lost or stolen property in the area, and give a full description of same. If the pawnbroker was to be offered these goods, he was to try to detain the person pawning and call the Gardai. The pawnbroker was obliged to store goods properly. No one was allowed to alter engravings or identifying marks on silverware and so forth. Pawnbrokers could also be called before the courts to explain their records. Any frivolous complaints, however, would result in the complainant having to compensate the pawnbroker for up to £10. The Gardai were allowed to inspect pawnshops at any time, and impound goods. It was an offence to obstruct Gardai in so doing.

THE 1995 ACT

Part fifteen of the *Consumer Credit Act* of 1995 amended the 1964 *Pawnbrokers Act*. An application for a pawnbroker's licence was to be made to the Director of Consumer Affairs, together with a fee of £1,000. The application could be turned down, much like in the 1964 Act, if evidence was forthcoming showing the person was not fit to open a pawnshop, if he was financially unsound, if he held a bookmaker's, intoxicating liquor, gaming, moneylender's or auctioneer's licence, if he had a criminal record during the previous five years, or if his premises was deemed unsuitable for carrying on a pawnbroking business. This Act ordered that a pawnbroker's licence would be valid for twelve months at a time, or at any time the Director of Consumer Affairs may choose to terminate it for failing to comply with any of the conditions.

If the licence was refused or terminated, the applicant or the holder of the licence could appeal to the Circuit Court. A pawnbroker's licence could be transferred, providing all conditions were met, and a fee of £500 was submitted .

This is the last major legislation on the pawnbroking trade in the Republic of Ireland. Pawnbrokers in Northern Ireland are now governed by United Kingdom laws, which lie beyond the scope of this book.

There was another pawnbroking system in Ireland though, which we cannot overlook, and that is the Charity Pawnshop.

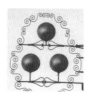

Chapter Eleven

THE CHARITY PAWNSHOP

Come away, poverty's catching.   Aphra Behn (1640-1689)

Pawnbrokers trading in Ireland at present are commercial pawnbrokers; that is, they conduct a commercial activity. Any profits are theirs, as are any losses. But at one time, trading simultaneously alongside the commercial pawnshops were alternative pawnshops, the Charity Pawnshops, called the *Mont De Piété* (from French, meaning Banks or Mountains of Pity). The last attempt at these ventures survived only a few difficult years in Ireland, but their presence brought about new improvements in a trade that was fast being tarnished by a small number of corrupt and greedy individuals, who thought nothing of cheating the poor and riding roughshod over the laws that were meant to protect them.

The origins of the *Mont De Piété* can be traced back many centuries before, to the Emperor Augustus, who lived just prior to the birth of Christ. He established a fund out of property confiscated from criminals, and accordingly lent money from these funds to the poor, without interest. Later, Tiberius did something similar, as did Alexander Severus who lent money at very low rates of interest to enable the poor purchase land. At the arrival of Christianity, the churches collected gifts, and used money to help the needy. The money was lent, at first without interest, provided pledges were deposited as security. Then loans were extended to those who were on the verge of poverty unless they obtained loans. Nominal loan interest was charged.

A long-running dispute arose within the Church as to the morality of charging interest, until the Papal Bull at the Fifth Lateran Council in the fifteenth century (see chapter two), which found in favour of those wishing to change. From then on, all cities in Italy quickly, and without fear of Church condemnation, opened up these lending houses. This was an enormous relief, as a depression in Europe in the fourteenth and fifteenth centuries had meant higher interest rates from moneylenders. There was a resulting backlash against the moneylenders, who were considered greedy and usurers in all but name.

A Franciscan, Barnabas Interamnensis of Terni, who saw the practices of Jewish moneylenders in particular as harmful to society, is often credited with opening the world's first Mons Pietatis (as it was called in Italy), a low-interest or interest-free lending house, on 13 January, 1463 at Perugia. In actual fact, the credit must be shared with friars Michael Carcano and Fortuna Coppoli, who put the theory into practice, after Barnabas and Antony of Todi revealed that they had a vision of Christ instructing them to 'make a mount (*mons*)'. There is notable irony in their effort to raise initial capital: the friars had to borrow 1,200 florins from Jewish moneylenders. Soon afterwards, Terni itself in 1464, Siena in 1472, Assisi in 1485 and a year later Florence, were just some of branches opening in Italy. Civic grants, public subscriptions or taxation raised the initial capital. The *depositarius* ran the *Monte*, a *conservator* looked after pledges, a *notarius* kept the books, a *trombetta* announced the sale of unredeemed pledges and a *venditor* was the auctioneer. These gave their services free of charge or at a very minor fee.

Compared to other moneylenders, the *Monte* were a vast improvement. The Florentine branch, for instance, charged six per cent on loans, much lower than rates charged by pawnbrokers, which was anything between 32 per cent and 44 per cent.

This had an impact on the Lombards, who had replaced the Jews as moneylenders in thirteenth-century Italy when the Jews were ostracised for usury. But some branches ran out of money or people just did not support them.

The movement was then greatly helped by the drive of fellow Franciscan, the renowned orator ('when he attacks vice, he does not speak – he thunders and lightens') Bernardine of Feltre. Born Martin Tomitano in Venezia, Italy, in 1439, Bernardine (who, incidentally, is the patron of pawnbrokers, his feast day being celebrated on 28 September) travelled afar to minister and preach against sin, including usury, and pressed for the setting up of these charity pawnshops. As a result, further establishments came into being.

The *Monti*, though, were mainly for town people, and rural communities had to rely on the Lombards, Cahorsins or others for loans. Despite opposition from Jews (and indeed many Christian religious leaders who were still opposed to the concept of charging any interest), more and more *Monti* opened. They were by now in places such as Nuremberg in Germany (1498). It was not until 1539 that Rome saw its first lending house opened, whilst later Amsterdam (1568), Brussels (1619), and Paris (1626) followed suit. That particular Parisian establishment lasted only a year, but a lending house reopened in the French capital in 1777.

Similar municipally-supervised pawnshops such as *Positos* in Spain, *Bank Van Leening* in Amsterdam (1614), and *Riksens Standers Bank* in Stockholm were established soon after. Attempts had been made to open charitable pawnshops in Britain on several occasions but without success. In 1707, Queen Anne granted permission to open a 'Charitable Corporation for the relief of the industrious poor, by assisting them with small sums upon pledges at legal interest'. This traded and indeed lasted until the 1730s, but it closed shortly afterwards due to bad management.

The *Monte Piété* system appears to have already been firmly established in Ireland in the early eighteenth century, and may even have been established before then, as there is a record of a

County Mayo Franciscan friary, *Montes Piétati* (the exact site is unclear, but possibly at Killedan, near Kiltimagh) in 1646. This certainly suggests a charity pawnshop in existence there, but hard evidence of how it operated seems to be missing. There are documents referring to the Mayo *Monte Piété*, dating from May 1719, in the hands of the Franciscans in Dublin, with names of various *guardiani* of the Monte recorded, ranging from Franciscus French in 1746 to Hubertus McNally in 1836. Fr McNally was evidently the last before the establishment closed, for from 1837 onwards the *Montes* was noted as 'vacant'.

When, in the eighteenth century, Dr Sam Madden had proposed that a charitable pawnshop system be started in Ireland, he strangely ignored that one apparently been operating simultaneously west of the Shannon. Or did he? Could this mean that the Mayo friary, named *Montes Pietatis*, was just given that name, without actually fulfilling the roll of a charity pawnshop? This is certainly possible, given the lowly populated area in its vicinity. But evidence to the contrary may be based on the activites of a young Limerick man named Matthew Barrington.

The Parisian *Mont De Piété* system had caught the eye of

The Barringtons, including Matthew, second from left.

Barrington as he sought ways to raise funds for his father's hospital. Born in 1788 (ironically the same year as the second *Pawnbrokers Act* in Ireland), Matthew trained as a lawyer, attaining the position of Crown Solicitor for Munster at the age of only 26. He married that same year, to Charlotte Hartigan. The couple bought a large estate soon afterwards in East Limerick, and built on it Glenstal Castle (now Glenstal Abbey, occupied by Benedictine monks). In 1829, Matthew's father, Joseph, opened a much-needed hospital in Limerick city. Running Barrington's Hospital needed no little funding, so Matthew, aware of the success elsewhere in Europe of the charity pawnshops in financing hospitals, decided that the time was right to open a *Mont De Piété* to achieve this aim, and also to relieve the pressures on the poor whom, he believed, were being unfairly treated by commercial pawnshops. In 1824 another attempt had been made to open a Charitable Pawnshop system in England, but it was unsuccessful.

This did not dispirit Matthew. With the twin motives of helping the poor and raising hospital funding, Matthew approached

Barringtons' Hospital, which was partly funded by the charity pawnshop.

the project with vigour. He wrote to the House of Commons in 1835 asking for the setting up of the *Monti*. He used the success of elsewhere as his argument, how it had helped build bridges, aqueducts and of course hospitals. Barrington argued that although efforts were made to bring the *Mont de Piété* to Britain and

Limerick's Mont de Piété, adjacent to Barringtons' Hospital.

Ireland before without success (including something not unlike a charity pawnshop back in 1361), there was no reason that on this occasion they would not thrive. Matthew's lobbying worked. Legislation was passed and he raised £4,000 to build an extension on to the hospital, an ornate building, with a cupola and classical pillars. Barrington's *Mont de Piété* finally opened for business in 1837. This date is important, for, as we saw earlier, the last guardian of the Mayo *Monte* was in that same year. Might we believe that the Franciscans, envisaging that the Barrington initiative would result in many such pawnshops establishing all over the country, decided to close their own *Monte*, and thence allow their friars to be released to other duties? It certainly is possible, but it is no more than an intelligent guess.

As 1836 drew to a close, Matthew Barrington proceeded with his own preparations in Limerick. Opening day was soon upon him and his staff, as a contemporary notice put it:

Business will commence about the 1st of January, 1837. The office will open at 10 o'clock each day, Sundays excepted, and close from March to September at 6, and from September to March at 4 0'clock.

How did Barrington's *Mont De Piété* work? There was no need to lodge bonds, as required by commercial pawnbrokers. Once the capital was raised (through debentures ranging from £5 to £100), the running of the *Mont De Piété* in Limerick was overseen by a committee of sixteen people, including two bishops, two MP's, the Mayor and the Chief Magistrate of Police. The day-to-day activities were managed by two people appointed by the committee. The Conductor (who had to be a licensed pawnbroker) had sole charge and responsibility for valuing the goods brought in to pawn, as well as storage arrangements. He received weekly cheques from the committee to cover cash outlay on pledges. The Inspector/Secretary responsibilities included inspecting the establishment daily, the books and correspondence. These men hired staff for the shop - twelve were hired initially, mostly youths aged between fourteen and eighteen. They were runners, clerks, porters, valuators, storekeepers and watchmen. Wages ranged from five to fourteen shillings per week. Total wages came to about £39 a month.

The policy of the *Mont De Piété* was to charge customers as little interest as possible. For example, in the case of a twelve-

Farthing token of the Mont de Piété, 1837.

shilling loan, the total cost extra to release goods in pledge would be two and a half pence. In comparison, it would cost the pawner five pence from a commercial pawnshop. The *Mont De Piété* did not charge for the issuing of a pawn ticket, or for affidavits when tickets were reported lost. When pawn tickets were reported lost, the Conductor issued a stop-ticket, which prevented anyone else trying to redeem the goods. On loans, the *Mont De Piété* adopted a policy of lending 80 per cent of the value on any gold, silver and jewellery, whilst they gave 66 per cent on all other pledges. *Mont De Piété* auctions of unredeemed pledges were to be advertised at least fourteen days in advance of the auction. The auctions were to be supervised by a staff member of the *Mont De Piété*. Whomsoever purchased goods at the auction had to pay up to five per cent of the selling

An example of an 1804 token from a Dublin pawnshop.

price as commission to the auctioneer. A one per cent levy was payable on any overplus. An overplus could be claimed by the pawner within the following two years. Pawn tickets issued by the *Mont De Piété* were a different colour every year. It was white in 1837 and green the next year. It also issued it's own tokens, or coins, which were issued to people who wanted to leave money in safe keeping with the establishment. The amount of interest was agreed upon by the owner and the Governors.

A clause in the *Loan Societies Act* of 1836 allowed the *Mont De Piété* to advance loans to fishermen within the local branch's county. The security required of the fishermen was a boat or fishing vessel, and the maximum loan given was no more than one half the value of the vessel.

The customers of the *Monte De Piété* also included huxters who sold eggs and potatoes. These pledged bedclothes in the morning to buy, perhaps, 8lbs of potatoes, which they sold in the evening to people who could not come to town during the day and so buy cheaper from farmers. The huxters made a nice profit and redeemed their goods from the pawnshop again.

The *Mont De Piété* also gave loans to people who wanted to buy cheaply from farmers and not have to pay more to the huxters that evening.

Despite the preparation and optimism at the start, the organisation soon found itself in difficulty. Plans were in place to open branches in Dublin, Cork, Youghal, Thurles, and Tandaragee in Armagh, but the brains behind the *Mont De Piété* in Limerick were worried. They banked on people flocking from the commercial pawnshops, where interest rates and overall charges were higher.

They also anticipated support for the upkeep of a hospital which was crucial to the life of Limerick. The fact that customers were charged less in the *Mont De Piété* can readily be seen from records of the time. Although the charges in English pawnshops were lower again than the *Mont De Piété*, the latter could never be accused of turning away customers in its Irish pawnbroking battlefield because of excessive charges. Whilst people may have come in their droves initially to the *Mont De Piété*, maybe because of Matthew Barrington, a highly respected man in Ireland at the time, and perhaps only for that reason, the trend reversed quickly. In the four years between 1837 and 1841, £78,595 was lent and only £71,005 received through the redeeming of pawns – nearly £8,000 of a shortfall, which was considerable in those days. The hospital had to rely more and more on charity sermons to obtain income.

Why then did the people not continue to support the *Mont De Piété*? The answers appear to be simple enough. Firstly, as stated, the novelty of Barrington's name wore off. People soon wanted more than just that. Secondly, the *Mont* might have charged low interest and no fees, but they also could not afford to issue loans as large as the other pawnshops. They planned to issue larger loans in time, for sure, but time was a luxury they could not afford. Management at the *Mont De Piété* were reluctant to drop interest charges much in case it ruined the business of commercial pawnshops. Ironic, since the latter did not reciprocate the concern when the *Mont* was in trouble. The poor people therefore simply returned to any pawnshop where they got larger loans, inevitably the commercial pawnshop. They did not worry about interest until another day.

Another difficulty for the Monte was of a practical nature. To get as large a loan as available from commercial pawnshops, people usually had to bring more goods with them to pledge, goods that were often quite heavy. It is easy to forget that the vast majority of people had to walk everywhere then. People were understandably reluctant to carry heavy goods for a long distance if there was an easier way. What had happened to some branches in Italy in the fifteenth century – lack of public support – was now happening in Ireland.

With the combination of all the above factors, the *Mont De Piété*, which forced the closure of some commercial pawnshops initially (whose owners feared the competition and moved elsewhere), soon headed for doom. Branches did open in places like 46 Capel Street, Dublin, in 1840 (to help fund St Vincent's Hospital). It is known that the Foundress of the Sisters of the Holy Faith, Margaret Louisa Aylward (1810-1889), worked for a time in a branch of the *Mont De Piété* in Waterford. The *City of Cork Mont De Piété* was established in 1841, with offices at Academy Street, Barrack Street and Mallow Lane. Its tokens had *Cork Mont De Piété Token* on one side and the Cork coat of arms on the other. In 1843, only three *Montes* traded in Ireland, including one at Portadown, but these too were soon in trouble and closed. The charity sermons organised as fund-raisers were not enough to foil the inevitable at Limerick, the Irish spiritual home of this most noble of pawning systems. The *Mont De Piété* at Barrington's Hospital was forced to close. At a board meeting on 6 December 1845, it was:

Resolved that having taken into consideration the propositions submitted for our consideration, we are of the opinion that the wards hitherto used for the purposes of the *Mont De Piété* be appropriated for the reception of convalescent patients discharged from the Fever Hospital for the present.

In 1847, it became a police barracks, and this attractive temple-like structure was demolished in 1892, its copper dome fetching a small fortune and its stone pillars ending up in New York.

And so ended the dream of Matthew Barrington. He died in 1861. Barrington's Hospital in Limerick lasted more than another century, closing in 1988.

Chapter Twelve

FAMINE AND PAWNING

There are two hundred million poor in the world who would gladly take the vow of poverty if they could eat, dress and have a home like myself and many of those who profess the vow of poverty.

Fulton Sheen (1895-1979)

In Ireland, when we mention famine, we usually think of that devastating period between 1845 and 1849, a period known as the Great Famine, when vast numbers succumbed to disease and death due to starvation. It has huge significance in our history, and was an event that had implications far beyond our shores, notably in America, where so many Irish went in search of a new life and helped to build that most powerful of countries. There were other famines in the story of Ireland too which caused destitution and death, albeit to a far lesser degree, like that of 1727, graphically described by Swift: 'That vast number of poor people who are aged, diseased or maimed ... every day dying and rotting by cold and famine and filth and vermin', and the famine of 1740/1 where: 'whole villages were dispeopled ... whole parishes were almost desolate, the dead were eaten in the fields by dogs.'

Chronic shortage was felt many other times, such as in 1755, 1757, 1766, 1770, 1782/3, 1800/1, 1816/18, 1822 and 1831.

As we can see, famines occurred several times in that century. This unwelcome reoccurrence of grave need resulted in more

hardship than usual. People were forced to try desperate measures to feed themselves and their families. Legal and illegal
methods were used. The pawning of what little people had, and
this more frequently than might have otherwise been the case,
just to get the bare essentials, was one of the first decisions made.

To get an overall picture of the impact of pawning in times of
particular need, we will look at the two most recent 'Great
Hungers' in Ireland: the Great Famine of 1845, and the near repeat
in 1879/90.

In 1844, on the eve of the Great Famine, the number of registered pawnshops in Ireland had risen to 467. These figures reflect-
ed a steady growth in the trade, and this trend looked set to continue. Why not, after all? 1845 would start no different to any
other year. Certainly, there was much shortage, but was not this
always the case? The poorest people would get by as usual – survival and no more. One of the means was pawning. The spring
and summer of 1845 were nothing extraordinary. Then disaster
struck. The first sign of the potato blight came in the autumn of
1845. Although it had been attacking potatoes in North America
for some time, the disease *Phytophthora infestans*, when it reached
Europe, took everyone by surprise. It was noticed in Belgium in
June, then the Netherlands and France by August, and the first
worrying reports of its sighting in Ireland came in September.
Newspapers played down the disease initially, but soon the evidence was clear. The blight was ruining virtually every potato in
the land, and the bulk of the population, who had come to
depend almost exclusively on this food faced starvation.

After the initial shock people thought, we will get over this,
we will go to the nearest pawnshop. We might be hungrier than
usual, but surely that won't last, will it? If they could get over
these few months, they felt, next year's potato crop would be
there, as healthy as ever. The pawnbroker would help them over
this trouble, as ever.

Meanwhile, those in the pawnbroking trade could not believe
their luck. On a humanitarian level the famine was an awful

curse. From a commercial point of view, a big increase in pledging, as happened in 1845, meant once the initial fright was over, that everyone would redeem their goods and a nice profit would ensue for pawnbrokers. So if misery saw out 1845, 1846 came and with it new hope. Everyone anticipated a good potato crop. They dared not think of the alternative.

What horror they must have felt when, after barely surviving 1845, they realised that the terrible disease raised its head again. Even the pawnbroker was becoming worried. Whilst it may have benefited him initially as he took in pledges as never before, the situation drastically worsened into nightmare proportions. No one was redeeming. They could not afford to. All the pawnbroker's money was out with the starving, who had spent it as quickly as they could to pay for extremely short-term succour. The pawnbroker had his goods, but what use was that to him gathering dust? The same pawnbrokers who had been loaning money to poor people were themselves now running into problems. William Forster, a Quaker who travelled over from London to offer his services to famine victims, noted:

> These pawnbrokers, who were the most prosperous looking I had seen on my journey, were, however, full of complaints against the times; there were, they said, no buyers, all were borrowers, their capital was all locked up, and soon they would be obliged to close their shops.

Some were forced to close down. Others followed the thousands who, with heavy hearts, headed for Queenstown or other ports to emigrate. Thomas Cinnamond, a pawnbroker from Belfast, had emigrated some twelve months earlier, before the potato crop failed. Many more were now forced to follow. If the traffic out of Ireland was in people, the incoming traffic was often in clothing. Cleanliness in times of extreme poverty was nearly impossible, so when second-hand clothing was imported into Ireland as relief, with them came germs and disease. These items of clothing were bought cheaply, carrying sickness into homes already threatened with hunger-induced illnesses. These clothes were then pawned as the situation worsened, so not only the people wearing them were struck down, occasionally pawnbrokers and their staff were too.

Reports of widescale and hitherto unsurpassed levels of pawning are very evident from surviving records of that era. In Athy, County Kildare, in 1846, people had 'pawned everything and cannot bear it much longer'.

Also in 1846, at Fermoy, a pawnbroker reported an increase in pledges, blaming it on the destitution. West of the Shannon, Higgins' pawnshop in Ballina showed that 23,456 items were pledged and about two-thirds were redeemed that same year. The next two years, however, were drastically different in the same pawnshop. In 1847, 27,448 items were pledged, and only 5,752 redeemed. In 1848, 24,805 items were pledged and only 5,206 redeemed, showing that the majority of people had no money to redeem what they had pawned. Godfrey Massey, Church of Ireland vicar at Bruff, County Limerick, found that from nearly 15,000 people in his area, nearly all Catholic:

7,000 were dying by inches, and almost naked for they had pawned or sold their little rags of clothes to keep the breath of life in themselves.

Lord Dufferin and G.F. Boyle visited Skibbereen in 1847:

The poor had pawned nearly every article ... many have parted with the means of future subsistence, as in the case of some fishermen, who have pawned their boats and nets.

This action of pawning the essentials of the fishermen's trade was noted around the coast. Of Claddagh, County Galway, William Forster stated:

Even the very nets and tackling of these poor fishermen, I heard, were pawned; and unless they be assisted to redeem them, they will be unable to take advantage of the herring shoals, even when they approach their coast. In order to ascertain the truth of this statement, I went into two or three of the largest pawnshops, the owners of which fully confirmed it, and said they had in pledge at least £1,000 worth of such property, and saw no likelihood of its being redeemed.

At Ring, at Bellmullet, at Killybegs and elsewhere, the situation was the same. Everything pledged, with no means to catch fish as they came near shore. The Society of Friends (or Quakers) helped enormously at the time by giving money, over £1,000, to fishermen to redeem such nets and tackle from pawnshops. In June of 1847, £50 was handed over by them to help fishermen in Arklow redeem 161 nets from pawn. There were 160 families were helped by this, and the first night's catch alone paid off the loan and more. Another problem facing the Quakers and those trying to assist the famine victims was the distribution of food. Initially food was given out uncooked, but people often pawned this, turning their situation from bad to worse. It was decided to pre-cook the food for distribution as a result. Similarly with clothing. Forster realised that it was necessary to make it more difficult for people to pawn clothing:

I found that the poor peasants, even for a considerable distance, were pledging their clothing for the most trifling sums; but after close enquiry, I satisfied myself that the coarse woollen and cotton garments which it is proposed to give to the more destitute, would not, *if stamped,* be articles which the [pawn]brokers would like to receive in pawn.

At Kilmactigue in North Connacht, in May of 1847, Mrs Jones, a Quaker, noted:

Nothing short of starvation would induce the peasantry of this neighbourhood to sell or pawn their clothes. Many consider it a disgrace to do so. However, within the last winter many have done so in every family. One woman pawned her shawl to give bread to her family.

The Society of Saint Vincent De Paul, in January of that same year, stated :

> besides the fullest allowance of bread, meal, and soup, we think the Society might reasonably advance to redeem pledged clothes and pay the rent (one shilling a week) for those utterly destitute outcasts.

The same Society reported later in Limerick that a young woman, though religious, had been unable to attend Mass for over a year because her clothing was in pawn.

The building of railway lines in Ireland at the time helped some from starvation and death, as is evident from the following: 'the reason of the increase of pledging in these four months (January to April 1847 in County Westmeath) is in consequence of the number employed at the railway ...'

In 1848, the stoppage of work on the Mullingar line meant more pledging, again simply to get money. In 1848 too, Finegan's pawnshop in Mullingar reported: 'the peasantry are worse clothed than formerly. The class of people now pawning are the small shopkeepers and small farmers.'

In 1848, there was not a single pawnbroker in Oldcastle Union, covering Meath, Westmeath and Cavan, according to the Clerk of the Union, Mr Flanagan: 'there is no necessity for a pawn-office here ... for I am convinced that the entire clothing of a family, on an average of circumstances would not bring five shillings.'

John McDonnell, pawnbroker in Athlone, stated: 'a great portion of the sales for the past four years have been to persons emigrating to America, most of whom get an outfit previous to leaving the country.'

In Tralee, again in the same year, a pawnshop was: 'filled with wearing apparel of every description, home-made clothing materials, feather beds, bedding and tradesmen's tools of every kind.'

A letter in *The Telegraph* in late December from Patrick Hogan, a pawnbroker at Westport, describes: 'living skeletons, the saddest spectacle ever witnessed in any country or by any government [who] from necessity are compelled to deposit their wearing apparel in pawn.'

In Roscommon Union 1849, Mr Sharkey, pawnbroker and Clerk of the Union, revealed that:

> There is no difference in the description of properties pawned now and five years since; but there is a marked difference in the different qualities of the articles – for the reason that the poor, who used to pawn heretofore, have now no property to pawn; and that the persons who are now pawning, have better articles than the former poor had, there is less money lent now than heretofore on the articles; there is as much property pawned now as at any former period ... On the whole, it is very probable that pawnbroking must become extinct for want of purchasers for the forfeited goods.

This understandable pessimism for the future of pawnbroking proved unfounded, as finally, in 1849, the country was saved further agony with a healthy potato crop, and slowly goods were beginning to be redeemed and purchased from pawnshops.

How, then, does the reputation of the pawnbroker come out of the Great Famine? Whilst the gombeenmen – the traders and moneylenders who hiked up prices to exploit the starving – were reviled, pawnbrokers during the Great Famine must have been a help, until even they, when the situation was at its worst, could help no more. Pawnbroking did not thrive during the Famine. Between 1846 and 1847, the number of tickets issued had dropped by a third. Pawnbroking survived rather than thrived. Few escaped from the calamity.

Did pawnbrokers exploit the poor? Perhaps some did, especially the illegal pawnbrokers who ignored the regulations set up in 1786 and afterwards. In Galway, Campbell Foster, in 1846, had found:

> So little do the people know of the commercial value of money that they are constantly in the habit of pawning it. I was so incredulous of this that the gentleman who informed me asked me to go with him to any pawnbrokers to assure myself of the fact; and I went with him and another gentleman to a pawnbroker's shop kept by Mr Murray in Galway. On asking the question the shopman said it was quite a common thing to have money pawned; and he produced a drawer containing a £10 Bank of Ireland note pawned six months ago for 10/-; a 30/-; Bank of Ireland note pawned for 1/-; a £1 Provincial Bank note pawned for 6/-; and a guinea in gold, of the reign of George III, pawned for 15/- two months ago.

Perhaps there were valid reasons for pledging money (as a safe place for deposit maybe?), and that Forster was underestimating the awareness of the people, but one imagines that the Galway pawnbroker would have explained this to the visitor if it were true. If indeed it was the case that certain pawnbrokers took advantage of the poor, it was unlikely to have been widespread. There were, after all, incidents of riots when people reached desperation in their quest for food, so would this not have also happened if pawnbrokers were discovered to have cheated their customers, and deprived them of means for food? Some might argue that pawnbrokers should not have accepted the pitiful clothes and bedding of the suffering population, but what could they as business people do? Pawnbrokers, if they wished to remain in business, relied on people pawning and redeeming. That was the nature of the business. By issuing loans, pawnbrokers at least succeeded in holding so many back from the precipice of death. If they were not there, how many more would have died we might ask.

The effect on pawnbroking during the Great Famine might

best be summed up by Cormac O'Grada:

> Did pawnbroking thrive during the Famine? The answer is a pretty emphatic no. The aggregate number of legal pawn tickets fell by over one-fifth between 1846 and 1847, and the total lent by almost one-third. Neither those numbers nor individual accounts support the notion that the famine was a golden opportunity for pawnbrokers.

Once the Great Famine was over, people cautiously got back to normality believing there was no danger of this nightmare being allowed to happen again.

Yet less than twenty years later Ireland nearly experienced a second Great Famine.

In 1879, trouble loomed. The signs were ominous. Several years of poor harvest left people with less and less to fall back on should circumstances deteriorate. The tillage acreage had been reduced. The wheat culture was ruined.

In 1846, when this country had 8,500,000 population, we were exporting £6,000,000 worth of cereals; in 1879 we had to import over £8,000,000 worth of the same produce to feed a population one-third less than it was then, commented Dublin Corporation.

The Cork Butter Market and the Tipperary Market were showing a significant reduction in production and prices. Everything seemed to be going wrong. And then echoes of 1845 – dreary, wet weather (the wettest on record until then) made conditions right to rot corn and infest potatoes with blight. Two-thirds of the potato crop was useless for a people which still depended on same for nourishment. So soon after the Great Famine, all feared that unless measures were taken to help people hit by the failed harvest, another catastrophe would ensue. Appeals were made to landlords to make allowances for delays of people in paying rent, and for the Government to back this up with legislation. The Government ignored those demands, but landlords did fortunately listen to pleas. Relief measures were set up, chiefly through the Dublin Mansion House Committee which was given the task to distribute much of funds collected to relieve the hardship. Help came from all over Ireland as well as from Britain, France, Asia, Australasia and America. The relief never took the form of money – it was food, fuel or clothing.

Information on conditions around the country showed how much dependency there was on pawning. Fr Peter Harte of Ballina, County Mayo, told the Committee:

> They have nothing now to live on, I might say, but Indian meal, and not enough of; some of them without a drop of milk, without fuel, and all without credit, having their clothes pawned and their children half naked.

From Castlree, County Roscommon, Rector James Treanor revealed:

> Numbers of the unfortunate people in the parish have been compelled to pawn their clothes and bedding, so that, in addition to starvation that stares them in the face , they are suffering keenly from want of clothing.

The Parish Priest in Castlemaine, County Kerry, Father Cornelius Sheehan said:

> From my own personal knowledge I can certify to your Lordship that the bedclothes of numbers of them, and whatever other clothes the pawnbroker would take in pledge, are in pawn for their support.

From a correspondent with the *Freeman's Journal* in the west of Ireland came: 'nothing to sow, nothing to fish with, nothing to pawn.'

The *Daily Telegraph* reported much the same state of despair: 'a squatter, evicted from his farm, and living on a patch of conacre; potatoes gone since November, seeds and all living since by pawning; nothing now left to pawn.'

Further instances were filtering through to Dublin: 'to tell the truth, we haven't a rag or clothes to go to Mass, nor a blanket itself that is not in pawn.'

J.A. Fox reported from Mayo:

> bedding there is none, everything of that kind having long since gone to the pawn-office, as proved to me by numerous tickets placed in my hands for inspection in well-nigh every hovel. Yet, notwithstanding this desperate condition of things, the police informed me that there was no crime, small or great, and a retired sub-inspector of the Force pointed out a large house in Bellaghy, filled from floor to ceiling with the pawned goods of the poor, which, he added, was not even protected by the presence of anyone on the premises at night – such is the unimpaired honesty of this starving people.

Drs Sigerson and Kenny gave an instance in the west where a pregnant woman pawned her jacket and petticoat to pay for the fare of her husband to get to England for work.

The agony, mercifully, was not as acute or as long term as that experienced in the 1840s. Three main reasons are given for this – a smaller population, the ready availability of Indian meal, and a reduced dependency on the potato. Also, the Government was quicker than their predecessors in 1845 to take responsibility and organise relief.

Instead of another Great Famine, it became a 'crisis'. Few died. The Famine Relief worked and, in no small way again, pawnshops assisted those in need. It did not always happen though that pawnbrokers were so willing to put the plight of others before their own greed.

Chapter Thirteen

CORRUPTION IN IRISH PAWNBROKING

A thief believes everybody steals.   E. W. Howe (1853-1937)

Pawnbroking, rightly or wrongly, has never had a clean image. The introduction of regulations in the late eighteenth century was intended to eradicate the historic ills associated with pawnbroking, but this was to prove sadly mistaken.

In 1835, a special enquiry on Municipal Authorities in Ireland revealed disturbing problems with the pawn trade. Subsequently, within three years of this, a *Commission of Enquiry into Pawnbroking in Ireland* was established, and this was to expose some shocking and widespread corruption involving not only pawnbrokers, but also auctioneers and even senior officials of Dublin Corporation.

The Report was thorough. Even the seemingly trivial issue of the size and substance of pawn tickets came in for criticism (too flimsy and so easily lost). Yet the one big drawback from our perspective today is that no customers of pawnbrokers were asked for their views. All the evidence came from those within or associated in some way with the trade, or from department officials.

The Committee justified this exclusion by stating it was not:

> desirable to seek for much evidence as to the detailed cases of hardship which might be brought forward, in which poor persons may have been defrauded by pawnbrokers. Each individual case of that

kind which might be stated must be thoroughly investigated before it could be considered as established; and after it had been proved, at a considerable sacrifice of time and expense, it would probably be alleged to be but a solitary instance of misconduct, which ought not to prejudice the general character of the whole trade.

All the more amazing then when the attack on pawnbroking, and the individuals making a living from it was quite stinging. Every rule, it seemed, was being ignored by a certain element of the trade to the detriment of the man on the street.

What did offend those assigned to inquire into the laws and regulations which effect the trade of pawnbroking in Ireland and their practical operation?

Many pawnbrokers never kept a Releasing Book, so the authorities could not keep a proper check on the amount of loan interest charged. Many more kept all their books improperly, and if a customer wanted to see them, he would be told to ask the auctioneer, who might be miles away. When writing the amount of loans into their books, pawnbrokers manipulated the situation so that they could obtain more interest when pledges were redeemed. For instance, a loan of two shillings, which would

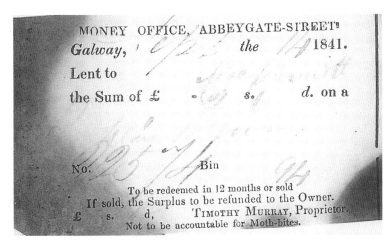

MONEY OFFICE, ABBEYGATE-STREET,
Galway,   the   1841.
Lent to
the Sum of £   s.   d. on a

No.   Bin

To be redeemed in 12 months or sold
If sold, the Surplus to be refunded to the Owner.
£   s.   d,   TIMOTHY MURRAY, Proprietor.
Not to be accountable for Moth-bites.

This burnt pre-famine pawnticket was found up a chimney more than a century later.

normally fetch one penny in interest, would be written in his books as a loan of two shillings and one penny, the penny bringing it above the threshold of two shillings and so the pawnbroker could charge his customer more again in redemption fees. Pawnbrokers overcharged for duplicate tickets too, and they traded outside the legal hours, facilitating thieves seeking to pawn stolen goods under cover of darkness and before the owners realised their possessions were missing. Pawnbrokers often sent pledges to be auctioned to auctioneers miles from town, making it extremely difficult for customers to travel to or even know about auctions. Some pawnbrokers, to avoid letting on that they were selling alcohol, registered pawnshops in their wife's name.

The Report revealed a strong suspicion that Dublin pawnbrokers paid a man in the Town Clerk's Office to return stolen goods to them rather than to the rightful owner. One pawnbroker from Carrickfergus had been imprisoned for refusing to give up a stolen coat pawned with him. Pawnbrokers often sold pledges over the counter, ignoring the fact that they had to send them to auction first. But even if every law in the book was broken, pawnbrokers were still allowed to trade once nominal punishment was endured. Only one pawnbroker, according to evidence given by George Mathews of the Central Loan Fund Board in Ireland, had his licence withdrawn due to failing to have the correct licence. The Report stated:

> There is no power, either in Dublin or elsewhere, of disqualifying a pawnbroker who may have repeatedly violated the most material provisions of the Act. His books may be perfectly unintelligible to the Magistrates; his frauds may be repeated; his shop may be open at improper hours; his forfeited pledges may be sold by private contract, and yet he may continue to take advantage of an Act which he disobeys.

Auctioneers came in for criticism too. It was revealed that they too often kept improper books, which not only prevented the pawners from collecting any excess or overplus after auctions, but also resulted in less duty for Customs and Excise. The Customs and Excise acknowledged that they did not have the manpower to police the auctioneering trade properly. The excise duty at auctions was payable by the purchaser. For example, on an item sold for four shillings, two pence was payable. There was a prevalence amongst auctioneers to make false declarations of accounts. The fine of £100 was worth the risk in their eyes. They also deliberately waited until minutes before the auctions started to show goods to the bidders, as, with the poor indoor lighting available in the mid-nineteenth century, bidders would neither have the time nor anyway adequate lighting to inspect goods for flaws. Auctioneers stated in their defence that pledges came from pawnbrokers without duplicate tickets attached, thus making it impossible to identify the owner when it came to an overplus. Although auctioneers were obliged to erect signs at their premises advising pawners that an overplus could be claimed for the pawnbroker, they rarely did so in case they would antagonise the pawnbroker who may then not hire them any more.

The Report criticised the state of auction rooms, being filthy and no place for any respectable person to attend. The 'jobbers' in attendance looked more like pickpockets. Auctioneers were supposed to hire bellmen to go around the streets and alert people to the forthcoming auction, but usually the actual date of the auction was not mentioned, only the 'first opportunity arising'. It revealed that auctioneers in Dublin had to pay the Marshal or Sword Bearer in Dublin £6 a week just for the privilege of auctioning unredeemed pledges, and that the Marshal of Dublin blackmailed such auctioneers to pay him more or else he would sub-let the auctioneering to someone who would.

The Marshal (John Judkin Butler, appointed in 1831 after the death of his predecessor, Mr Stanley) came in for some scathing criticism in the Report:

The manner in which successive Marshals of the City of Dublin have discharged the duties imposed upon them by the Act will be found by the evidence ... to have been exceedingly unsatisfactory.

Butler was elected to office by Dublin Corporation. Although it was an appointment that was to be reviewed, in reality it was for life and would have taken a lot of effort to dismiss him. As a result he became smug and untouchable. His salary was £1500 a year, plus fees of around £350 per annum from registration of pawnbrokers licences, £250 for issuing notices of sale of forfeited pledges and a further £312 from sub letting his auctioneering duties. Compare this to a salary of £1200 a year for one of the other auctioneers, who fulfilled his auctioneering duties in person.

The Marshal was supposed to charge five shillings for registering a pawnbroker, and fifteen shillings for the registration of a pawnbroker's securities. In reality he got more for these transactions. He was obliged to ensure that pawnbrokers were registered and made regular and proper Returns, but he was found to have totally failed in his duties. He used his position purely as a money-making venture. He rarely checked Returns, or if securities were lodged. He paid a man ten shillings a week to issue notices to pawnbrokers' customers, but never checked to see if he was doing his job. There seemed to be a nod and a wink arrangement between the Marshal and pawnbrokers. They sent up money to him at the start of the year, more than the twelve shillings required, once he did not ask questions, and the Marshal seemed quite happy to turn a blind eye. When confronted, the Marshal said he was just doing what his predecessor did. He even undermined the impartiality of his office by asking for loans from pawnbrokers when he was short of money. The list of complaints was long, but the Marshal was kept in office for a few more years and given a golden retirement income of £444 per annum.

Yet it was not all doom and gloom for the trade in the 1838 Enquiry. On the positive side, pawnbrokers, the Report stated, usually increased the size of their loans to attract people inside their premises to get more business. The Report also defended pawnbrokers for charging higher interest than say banks, because a lot of the time pawnbrokers money, in the form of pledges in their stores, was locked away, especially in summer, and to cover the costs of warehousing, they needed to levy money on customers at a higher rate than elsewhere, more particularly when items like clothing deteriorated in store and would fetch less money at auction.

Nevertheless praise was rare in the Enquiry.

Other points of interest in the Report give us a further insight into the trade. Dublin pawnbrokers, we learn, had a small fund to defend themselves against possible summonses. Summonses issued against the trade were decided upon at the Lord Mayor's Court of Conscience at Coppinger Row. The licence paid by pawnbrokers in Dublin went towards the expenses of Dublin City police. Pawnbrokers themselves argued for earlier opening hours, because this, they claimed, would do away with the need for men to lose a quarter day's pay when they had to wait until the 10am opening. The Report said that pawnbrokers usually hired auctioneers with whom they got the best deal, who may not have been the auctioneer nearest to them. Auctioneers fees at the times from pawnbrokers auctions were five per cent, plus expenses. Of the four appointed auctioneers in Dublin, the Sword Bearer sub let his auctioneering duties to another person for a fee of £321 per annum. The two auctioneers appointed by the Lord Lieutenant did not do this. Auctioneers usually held auctions more than once a week – in Antrim, an auctioneer held them four times a week, from 11am to 5pm. Others held theirs at night.

The Report stated that auctioneers usually waited for the room to fill up with bidders to ensure competition in prices, that they held auctions of jewellery at night, that auctioneers sold to 'jobbers' on credit (no cash changed hands at auctions). Bellmen at auctions received payment of one shilling a day and porters one shilling and six pence.

Outside Dublin, auctioneers, where appointed at all, were appointed by Grand Juries. These Grand Juries consisted of 24 of the biggest landowners in the county, who had legal duties which included raising funds by levying taxes on land occupiers. The auctions themselves took place in the pawnbroker's premises. Auctioneers, when they were not selling for pawnbrokers, auctioned furniture and household goods.

The Committee concluded the Report trusting:

> that much of the odium and discredit attached to the trade at present will be removed, and that those persons of character who embark in it may introduce into the business a more wholesome species of competition than has yet been seen.

In 1868, the Government felt the need to launch another enquiry. A new *Pawnbroking Inquiry Commission* was appointed by the Lord Lieutenant to inquire into the improvements, if any, and state of the trade since before the Famine.

The Report revealed the hopes and intentions of the first Enquiry had not satisfactorily been realised, and that, still, all was not well in the trade. Martin Crean, the sitting Marshal of Dublin, in his evidence, stated that many pawnbrokers were still not lodging bonds, and refused to submit monthly Returns. The 40 shillings fine for this neglect was never enforced. Appraisers were not appointed by County Grand Juries as they were meant to be, so pawnbrokers could sell goods as they wished. He said Dublin pawnbrokers were holding auctions without notifying customers. They also sold goods in bundles which contained items belonging to different people, making it difficult for the owners to track down later when seeking overpluses. Francis Byrne, a Dublin pawnbroker, in his evidence, admitted that pawnbrokers stayed open longer than legally permitted.

Yet this was a different and, in many ways for the historian, less revealing type of Inquiry than its predecessor. Probing cross-examination of pawnbrokers, auctioneers and others (which excluded yet again pawnshop customers) does not appear to have taken place, or if it did, such questions did not appear in the finished Report. Criticism of the trade was modest, whilst recommendations to lift the restrictive laws imposed on pawnbrokers and auctioneers were strong. Maybe this is an indication that, after all, pawnbroking was by now a far more law-abiding business than hitherto. The recommendations from the Inquiry included:

change in legislation to allow far longer trading hours for pawnshops; the oath given by Dublin pawnbrokers to be abolished; the requirement for pawnbrokers to give securities be scrapped; the tax on Dublin pawnbrokers for the upkeep of the Dublin Metropolitan police be removed; laws allowing any auctioneer in Dublin to sell pawnbrokers unredeemed pledges be introduced, rather than just the four Divisional Auctioneers; the obligation for pawnbrokers to make Returns to parliament be abolished.

In time, most of the obstacles faced by pawnbrokers were removed or softened, as the trade gradually distanced itself from its more sordid past.

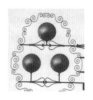

Chapter Fourteen

VOICES FROM BOTH SIDES OF THE COUNTER

Money is like muck, not good except it be spread.

Francis Bacon (1561-1626)

In the course of research, numerous people were interviewed and asked to share some of their memories of pawnshops. The following are some examples.

CUSTOMERS

'The things I remember most about pawnshops were the wooden floors and counters. Also the clothes being wrapped up in newspaper. A number was pinned on the bundle with a straight pin and then put on the shelves. First Holy Communion clothes were often pawned. You'd have them for a day or two and never see them again. Myself and my sister would be sent down with instructions to ask for say 7/6, knowing that you'd only be given 5 shillings. You'd be embarrassed alright going to the Pawn, but it was the times.'

'I got a watch for my Communion. My sister bought it. It had a black strap and chrome surround to the face. I loved it. My mother would often say to me 'here's sixpence for a loan of your watch'. I'd give it and she'd go to the Pawn.

I'd get it back at the end of the week. One day I was going to

2. **THIS IS A 4 MONTHS PLEDGE.**

3. After the expiration of that time the pledge may be sold by auction by the pawnbroker. But it may be redeemed by the pawner at any time before the day of sale.

4. Within twelve calendar months after sale the pawner may, on payment of a fee of six pence, inspect the account of the sale in the pawnbroker's book and in the auctioneer's catalogue and receive any surplus produced by the sale. If, however, within six months before or after that sale, the sale of another pledge or pledges of the same person has resulted in a deficit the pawnbroker is entitled to set off the deficit against the surplus.

5. If a pledge, through default, neglect, or wilful misbehavious on the part of the pawnbroker, is lost, destroyed or is of less value at the time of redemption than it was at the time of pawning, the pawner may apply to the District-Court for an order for compensation. The amount of compensation, if any, awarded shall be deducted from the sum payable to the pawnbroker or as the case may require, shall be paid by the pawnbroker in such manner as the Court may direct.

6. If the pledge is destroyed or damaged by fire the pawnbroker, if the pawn-ticker is tendered to him before the expiry of the period within which the pledge would have been redeemable, will be bound to pay an amount equal to one half of the amount of the loan, unless otherwise agreed upon by the pawner and pawnbroker.

7. If this ticket is lost or mislaid the pawner should at once apply to the pawnbroker for a form of declaration; otherwise the pawnbroker will be bound to deliver the pledge to any person who produces this ticket to him and claims to redeem the pledge.

**PLEASE INSURE
YOUR PROPERTY.**

....Pawnbroker

.... Pawner

An example of a four months pledge.

play a match and my mother said "why can't you leave your watch after you, you might lose it". I did and I never saw it again. Obviously my mother couldn't redeem it from the pawn.'

'I remember buying some things in the Pawn. Some 78 records, and one day a lovely transistor. I recall an old shawled woman looking at me spending £3 or so on the radio when she was handing in her pledge, probably just to make ends meet. I felt self-conscious.'

'As children we used to play pawnshop upstairs in our terraced house. We lived upstairs – Mam, Dad and six children. Our grandparents lived downstairs. We played Paddy the Pawn, as we called it, with our older brother being the pawnbroker. He'd be standing behind the table with paper and a pencil. We girls got a loan of a sheet from Mam and gave it to our brother, who gave us the pretend pawn ticket and more cut up paper for money. A few minutes later we'd return with the ticket and our money to redeem the sheet.'

'I'm an alcoholic, although I haven't touched a drink for 28 years. But when I did drink, I'd use the pawn often. Anything for money for the drink. I'd take my brother-in-law's razor and pawn it. He didn't know. My mother-in-law would buy it back from the pawnshop before he found out. Then I'd take it again. It happened all the time.'

'Everyone went to their own favourite clerk behind the counter, because they knew they'd get more for their pledge off him. You'd often accompany your mother to the Pawn, and in this way you'd get known, so when your mother couldn't go, you'd be known as her daughter and get the same deal. You'd be told, of course, "go to Finbarr" or whoever for the best deal. Mondays, Fridays and Saturdays were the busiest. There would be loads of people along the counter and a good lot of staff, maybe six. There was also a small counter for people who didn't want their business known.'

'The people who were embarrassed about going to the pawnshop might have brought their pledges under a shawl or fold it in brown paper and pretend they were going elsewhere. I knew a woman who used to get off the bus before her friend did, pretending she was going somewhere, only in reality she was going to the Pawn. Some were ashamed, but they had no reason to be. They weren't getting money under false pretences. Today you get loans of other people's money and you'd have to pay them back. Nothing is thought of that.'

'Without pawnshops people would have starved. The 1930s were very tough. Jobs weren't that plentiful. My father might get a casual day's work down the docks. His shoulders would be red raw from carrying the planks. Anyway, social welfare payments were very small, maybe only £1 a week, with thirteen shillings for two days work. That wasn't enough to feed the family, pay the rent and all that, so they had to pawn. They had no choice.'

'When the War started, men went to England and got work, and they sent money home every week. This was the first regular money into the house. People therefore didn't need to pledge, and in fact they started to redeem what they already had in pawn. This was the start of the end of pawnshops. After the war, jobs became easier to get, and children were growing up bringing more money into the home. The hire purchase and credit unions appeared then, and that really made a difference.'

'One Good Friday, my grandmother took me to the post office to draw out her old age pension. After leaving, she went straight across the road and bought us three lovely Easter eggs for four shillings. When she took us home, she took me aside and quietly asked me to pawn her lovely new apron. We came first you see. Times were tough. One Christmas, my mother made sure we had clothes and food, but we hadn't even coal for the fire. It makes me cry to think of it.'

'Women mostly pawned while the men were at work, or looking for work. Pension books were popular pawns. The goods for sale in pawnshops were displayed in the window and the rest were hanging up indoors. The clerk would use a long pole to get them down off the racks. People used to pawn mostly for food or to pay the rent. My mother often pawned her shawl. A Double Decker, it was called, great quality. She only brought that out for pawning.'

'A lot of people on our street had pawn tickets, and when I found I had none I was jealous. I felt our family were deprived.'

'Pawnshops were crowded, mostly with women. Everyone saw everyone else's dealings, but you accepted it. Everyone was in the same boat. Pawnshops were often smelly, but I'm not ashamed to admit my family used them. We had to.'

PAWNBROKERS

'Pawnbroking is the purest form of banking. It was a trade of its time. The era of the pawnshop is gone. I'm sad to see it go. It suited people's needs. There was nothing else then. It was a very upfront contract for both parties. The customer got money for goods. There was no credit.'

'There was a stigma attached to using a pawnshop, but that came mostly from the emerging middle classes. They wanted to distance themselves from their poorer past. None of us are far removed from the bog, though, are we?'

'Years ago, if you wanted a TV or car, you saved for them, but now you buy everything with loans or instalments, so there's nobody really without some borrowings. Pawnshops don't attract attention like they used to, because they are just another way of borrowing. The stigma has virtually died out. You go into any bank and ask for a loan, you're nearly asked what you had for your breakfast, so why should pawning be any more embarrassing?'

'You'd build up a relationship with your customer. There was a bond of trust. Once broken by either, that was it. Like in all businesses, you must trust them and they must trust you, or they won't come back. They'll just walk out the door and go somewhere else.'

'The first thing I was told when I entered the business as a young lad was that, although people may be poor, they may have no money, but what they did have was dignity, and that's the one thing you did not take from them. Remember, we made our money from these people. You didn't degrade them.'

'There would have been much easier ways to make money than through opening a pawnshop. What you mustn't forget is that a shopkeeper can buy goods on a Monday, sell them on a Tuesday, and have profit Tuesday night. The pawnbroker would have to keep the goods pledged for days, weeks or months before someone redeemed and gave him a profit. There was always that delay. You didn't have a quick turnover. It was always an uphill struggle.'

'We put Jeyes Fluid or a pine disinfectant on the floor every day. We used the same as was used in churches in the 1950s and 1960s. You'd mix the disinfectant with water, building up pressure and producing a very fine spray. This would keep the dust down as well as kill germs. They reckoned at one stage that two of the healthiest jobs around were working down the sewers and in pawnshops. Staff rarely had health problems – fleas alright, but that was it. Probably due to building up an immunity against disease.'

'My father was a pawnbroker. He used to come home on Saturday night at maybe ten o'clock because a lot of his clients were dockers or coal men and they didn't get paid until then. The pawnshops and many other shops in the street stayed open late for them.'

'People sometimes needed secure places to keep their goods, and pawnshops were cheaper storage than warehouses, whether it be a suit, wedding ring, pram or whatever. Once you had your pawn ticket, the contract was secure.'

'It was a job where you met an awful lot of people. People used to come in to our pawnshop who used their grandmothers surname, because she was known in the shop and her name stood for something. A lot of married women still used their maiden name. You knew people that way, you knew where they came from.'

'The pawnshop was ordinary – it wasn't a curiosity like it is now. It was like a pigs-head man or the undertaker, just another dot on the landscape, although a very important dot.'

'Basically what you had was racks for bundles. We'd fill a rack on Monday morning, the lower ticket numbers at the bottom. We'd keep goods there for a fortnight or three weeks and then move them upstairs. We had chutes from the top of the house right down to the counter. There was a string, and on top of the chute there was a bell. You'd ring and the ticket would be pulled up the chute by staff upstairs. The corresponding pledge would then be sent down the chute to the counter. The pledges were constantly moving, which kept them fresh from dust and helped air circulation.'

'The staff were usually from the locality. They knew the people. Most got the job through some customer who told that so and so needed a job, and that was how it happened.'

'You'd get the odd drunk coming in looking for money for drink, but we took care of them better than the publicans did. A bigger problem was when a group of young people would come in, with drink in them, and they'd try to intimidate you. The counters in our shops were higher to the customer than to the staff, however, making it hard for an unruly customer to attack staff.'

'If you had a suit in pawn and your husband, God forbid, died, you might have no money to redeem the suit. The undertaker might loan you the money to get it back from the pawn. Or the insurance man, he might give you a loan too.'

'Most goods are redeemed. Only a very small percentage goes to auction these days. That suits us. If everything was sure to be redeemed, we could lend more and then in turn get more interest. Ticket money is five per cent of the value of the goods, so overall we would benefit more by lending more.'

'A man once brought in a Viking bangle to pawn. He was digging the foundation for a bungalow down the country and he came across the bangle. It was over 1,000 years old. It was priceless. His uncle who owned the land hated anyone on his property, so the nephew kept the bangle in a drawer for years, and then decided to get rid of it. He wanted me to melt it, but I persuaded him to take it to the National Museum. I heard no more from the man, and I got a thank you later after a year from the Museum. Also, a fellow pawned a shrunken pagan head once, and that ended up in the Museum as well. They boiled the heads to shrink them. I didn't know what it was first, but it was genuine, from Irish pagan times.'

The following are extracts from a Dáil Éireann debate in February 1964, on the Second Stage of the Pawnbrokers Bill:

'It may be held by some that pawnbroking is dying out and that nothing should be done to keep it alive. I do not accept this view. Pawnbrokers have provided a very useful service to the community in the past. It is true that the statistics available reveal a steady decline over recent years in the demand for the services offered by pawnbrokers – a decline which reflects the general improvement in the level of wages and employment and expansion in credit facilities in other directions. Despite these improvements, however, I believe there will be room for the special loan facilities provided by pawnbrokers.' (*Charles Haughey, Minister for Justice*)

'The existence of the pawnbroker's establishment and its continued existence, even though in reduced numbers is, I think, a criticism of society, because ... the bulk of the people using these establishments still are unfortunate working-class mothers who are in serious need of absolute essentials ... This is not a criticism of pawnbrokers themselves because ... they provide a useful service, but a service which nobody should find himself in need of.' (*Dr Noel Browne, TD*)

'I think it is wrong that so many families do find it necessary to use the pawnbroker's establishment. It is essentially a sordid substitute for social justice and our people should not be placed in this position.' (*Dr Noel Browne,TD*)

'The pawnbrokers as such are a reputable body of law-abiding citizens.' (*Charles Haughey, Minister for Justice*)

'Pawnbroking in this country is, to some extent at any rate, a dying business.' (*M.J. O'Higgins, TD*)

'I certainly appreciate that for quite a considerable section of our people in the city of Dublin, pawnbrokers do provide an extremely useful service, and a useful service of a simple sort which enables poor people to raise a loan with a minimum amount of red tape and in the certainty that the article they are giving to the pawnbroker by way of a pledge can be redeemed.' (*M.J. O'Higgins TD*)

Chapter Fifteen

CONCLUSION

Perhaps against the odds, the pawnshop has thus far survived in Ireland. It has coped with the increased affluence of the population and the resulting reduction in the need for pawning. It has also withstood competition from an abundance of wealthier and more upmarket lending institutions which readily fulfil most of the needs of borrowers. Pawnbroking continues mainly, perhaps, because it has focused on its own niche in the market. It has wisely avoided trying to challenge the bigger players in a battle it cannot hope to win.

Pawnbrokers do not have thousands of shareholders or investors, nor have they the cushion of millions of pounds behind them, the amounts which make banks, building societies and others much bigger fish in the financial world. Pawnshops meet a different and often more pressing and immediate need, and that is their strength. They cater for the 'now' factor where, to reverse an advertisement line from many current financial advertisements, terms and conditions in general do *not* apply in relation to loans.

Pawnshops have also survived, perhaps, due to pawnbrokers willingness to adapt to the needs of the day. Where once clothes and pots and pans were the mainstay of their business, because people had little else to pawn, today it is jewellery (higher value, easier to sell and to store) and electrical goods. Where once a

A pawnshop sign (right of picture), in Barrack Street, Cork, some years ago!

shabby and dark shop went, for the most part, unnoticed and was rarely a deterrent to customers, today a bright and fresher appearance is required and expected.

In many respects, however, pawnbroking has changed little in centuries. A pledge is still handed up for evaluating and a loan is given. The resulting interest, repayments and eventual auctioning are subject to specific sets of laws to protect the customer and the pawnbroker, just like they have been for hundreds of years.

Yet there is no escaping the fact that there are now only a handful of pawnshops serving a population of over 3,000,000. Why is this so? Why, in larger urban areas like Cork, Galway, Kilkenny, Limerick and Waterford, do we find not one pawnshop? If an entrepreneur were adventurous enough to commence pawnbroking in any of these cities, might his business flourish or, on the other hand, rapidly die? What are the factors needed for pawnbroking, if not to thrive, at least to survive in the twenty-first century? I put these and related questions recently in Dublin to those who should know most – the latest in the long line of Irish pawnbrokers.

I noted on my visit how each of the four pawnshops ran a jewellery business from the same premises. Was this essential in order to survive?

'They compliment each other,' Pat Kearns, a Monaghan man who runs a pawnbroking business at Queen Street, replied. 'It would be tougher to run a pawnshop alone, but it would be possible.'

This was the opinion of Pat Carthy as well. He has two pawnshops – Kilbrides at Clanbrassil Street (the only pawnshop south of the River Liffey), and Carthys at Marlboro Street.

'My predecessor at Kilbrides ran a pawnshop alone, without retailing jewellery, and that was only five years ago, so it could be done,' noted Pat.

People might be of the opinion that a weak economy is good for pawnbroking, but is this correct?

Pat Kearns disagreed. He believed that neither a booming nor a depressed economy particularly helps his business. If you have a good economy, fewer people pawn, yet if the opposite occurs and the economy is weak, people will pledge but cannot afford to redeem their pledges. Pawnbrokers are thus handing out loans and getting little in return, and people cannot afford to purchase at auctions either. In between, in Pat's opinion, is better for the trade.

Regarding the need or opportunities for new pawnshops around the country, John Brereton, a pawnbroker at Capel Street, had this to say:

'There's probably a need for pawnshops, but the cost of starting up is very prohibitive. As well as the £1,000 licence, you also need an amount of money you have to invest in order to lend money. Then there's the capital and labour costs. You have the upkeep of a shop and all the responsibilities that go with it.

'It's not very remunerative. There are safer ways of setting up business. In the UK, more pawnshops are opening, but they can charge higher interest rates than here in Ireland.'

Pat Kearns, who concurred that there were easier ways of making a living than being a pawnbroker, pointed out a few more difficulties facing would-be pawnbrokers.

'Say if in Cork a pawnbroker opened a shop, people might get the idea that, without competition, the pawnbroker might abuse the situation and take advantage. He'd have a monopoly you see, and people might be reluctant to take their custom to him. With a few pawnshops, like here in Dublin at present, people can always go to another shop if either Pat, John or myself are not giving them as good a deal as they think fit. It would also be hard to open up afresh because there's a lot of trust involved, from the punters point of view.

'They are leaving in their valuables, items of sentimental value. If someone opened a pawnshop, and a customer handed in an engagement ring they had say for 50 years, if it's not a business with some association with the area or if the owner's not someone they know personally, the pawnshop could be gone overnight and the engagement ring lost to the customer forever. There's so many "fly-by-nights" that people are very wary.'

And of the future of pawnbroking in Ireland?

'The banks and credit unions are a threat to our business no doubt,' felt Pat Carthy 'but the Celtic Tiger hasn't helped a lot of people, so even the wealthiest of communities seem to need the pawnbroker and probably will for a long time to come.'

John Brereton agreed that pawning was not set for extinction just yet.

'Many middle-class people with high mortgages need pawnshops these days. They find it difficult to keep up with repayments, so they pawn.'

Pat Kearns also felt there was a future for the trade.

'You have the Celtic Tiger, but you also have house prices

going through the roof. Wages haven't gone up accordingly. At the moment people are stretched, and if the interest rates go up, then people will be in trouble. We've noticed we're getting pledges from new, private, housing estates. One particular estate up the country – you know people come from all over the country to pawn – is not even occupied, but some house owners there are pawning. We don't see as many tools being pawned lately, because tradesmen are so busy, but outside the building trade and the publicans, who else do you see the Celtic Tiger helping? Very few. Pawnbroking will, I expect, outlive the Celtic Tiger.'

Certainly, from my own limited experience in pawnshops, there seems to be a definite demand for pawnbroking in Ireland. Whilst interviewing John and the two Pats in their respective shops, for instance, there were plenty of people submitting pledges.

'How much do you want for it?'

'£50.'

'I'll give you £30.'

'Okay so.'

Jewellery mostly, but also a fishing rod and a guitar were pledged during my visit. I toured their stores where the pledges are kept and found all sorts of goods wrapped carefully and awaiting redemption. The atmosphere was polite and business-like in each shop. It did not seem to me in any way intimidating to the customer. In many respects, these modern day pawnshops are just like any other shop in any street in Ireland, offering a service which many choose to avail of. And as long as this is the case, pawnbroking should survive for a long time to come.

I've pawned a little,
I've pawned a lot,
I've pawned all I've needed,
I've pawned all I've got,
I've pawned my furniture,
I've pawned my clothes,
But for the pawnshop
God only knows.

Jim Fitzpatrick

Appendix A

Oath taken by Dublin Pawnbrokers 1788

I............ do swear that I will to the best of my understanding and ability, truly, faithfully and honestly exercise and carry on the business of a pawnbroker, pursuant to the several and respective clauses, regulations and alterations mentioned and set forth in this act, and also in said recited act, and that I will to the best of my knowledge, judgement and belief, make fair and true returns to the register of said business for the time being, of the number of sums I shall lend or cause to be lent in each calendar month, together with the sum total or amount of said sums. So help me God.

APPENDIX B

Oath taken by each of the four Divisional Auctioneers of Dublin in 1788:

I............ do swear that I will upon all occasions do justice to the utmost of my power, in the execution and discharge of the duties of my office as an auctioneer, and that I will upon the sale or sales of such goods as shall be committed to my care, bona fide, sell or cause the said goods to be sold, without any fraud, favour or collusion against, to or with any person or persons whatsoever, to the best and fairest bidders, and will enter, or cause to be entered, the exact and real price or prices for which the same shall be respectively sold, in order to render satisfaction to all such person and persons as shall be concerned or interested in the premises. So help me God.

APPENDIX C

A list of pawnbrokers trading in the main urban centres of Ireland in 1870, taken from Slaters Directory:

Belfast:

Aiken, Michael & Co., 76 Divis St
Allen, James, 111 Old Lodge Rd
Anderson, Henry, 17 Albion St
Anderson, Thomas, 59 Lancaster St
Anderson, Thomas, 9 & 11 Hemsworth st
Archibald, William & Co, 141 Bridge end, Ballymacarett
Beggs, John, 64 Cromac st
Cahoon, Robert, 13 Marquis St
Canning, Thomas, 55 Denmark St
Dickson, William, 6 Sandy Row,
Dobbs, John, 154 Shankill Rd,
Dreman, Nevan, 10 Boundary St
Dunn, Eliza Jane, 58 Curham St
Fee, Samuel, 86 Stanhope St
Fox, thomas, Ligoniel
Foy, Catherine, 31 Gt Patrick St
Galway, Arthur, 51 Shankill Rd,
Gamble, Arthur, 66 North Queen St
Giles, John, 24 and 83 Dock St
Gilmore, Thomas, 200 Old Lodge Rd
Gilmore, William, 27 Eliza St
Girvin, Joseph, 113 Peter's Hill
Girvin, Thomas, 34 Carrick Hill
Gordon, Jane, 1 and 3 Nile St
Gordon, Norris, 139 Durham St

Graham, Hugh & Co., 109 Bridge end
Gregory, Thomas, 27 Mount St
Griffith, James, 59 Donegall St
Hadskis, Abel, 169 North Queen St
Hamilton, Abraham, 47 Cromac St
Hanna, Samuel B., 11 Everton St
Harper, Hugh, 117 Shankill Rd
Hart, Francis, 43 Falls Rd
Hunter, William, 54 Falls Rd
Hunter, William, 36 Townsend St
Johnson, Henry, 40 Up. Townsend St
Jones, Joseph, 8 Garmoyle St
Keatley, Samuel, 1 & 3 Shankill Rd
Kelly, Edward, 33 Chapel lane
Kildea, Robert, 138 Cromac St
Kirker, Victor, 110 Cromac St
Lavery, Andrew, 60 Grattan St
Law, Robert, 193 Castlereagh St
Leathem, Joseph C., 211 Shankill Rd
Locke, Silas, 48 North Queen St
McAllen, Thomas, 97 Shankill Rd
McAuley, Hugh, 49 Albert Crescent
McCleery, James, 110 Nelson St
McConnell, Hugh, 72 Cullingtree Rd
McConnell, Frances, 144 Old Lodge Rd
McDonald, Francis, 5 Gt. Patrick St
McDonnell, Francis, 32 Church St
McDornan, John, 120 Durham St
McDornan, John Jn., 30 Williams Pl.
McDowell, John, 135 Old Lodge Rd
McGalwey, Peter, 26 Ardmoulin St
McKenna, Stephen, 14 Gt. Patrick St
McKeown, James, 34 John St
McKeown, William, Smithfield
McMillan, Samuel, 35 Henry St
McMillan, Anne, 67 Old Lodge Rd
Maguire, S. & Co., Chapel lane
Major, George, 6 & 8 Little Patrick St
Mann, Joseph, 1 & 3 William St South
Marshall, Alexander, 62 Academy St
Meek, Charles, 36 Earl St

Milliken, Robert, 60 Divis st
Minniece, Rebecca, 19 Sussex St
Morrison, Alex, 69 Shankill Rd
Morrow, Samuel, 113 Durham St
Mussen, William, 52 Carrick Hill
O'Hagan, John, Smithfield
Owen, William J., 42 Henry St
Owens, James B., 14 Barrack St
Scott, David, 183 North St
Scott, James, 201&203 Shankill Rd
Scott, John, 77 Peter's Hill
Scott, John, 101 Millfield
Smith, John, 81 Cromac St
Smyth, John, 55 Gt. Patrick St
Thorburn, Sarah, Little George's St
Todd, Henry, 42 Peter's Hill
Trimble, Samuel, 102 Falls Road,
Ward, Robert, 39 Lancaster St
Warnock, Joseph, 24 Robert St
White, John, 139 Nelson St
Whyte, William, 123 Wheeler's Pl
Whyte, William, 31 Union St
Wilson, James, 122 Sandy Row,
Wright, Andrew, 51 Ann St

Cork:

Adams, Ann, 84 North Main St
Bourke, Mary, 404 Blarney St
Browne, Patrick, 47 Clarence St
Burke, Edmond, 4 Shandon St
Busteed, Anne, 4 North Mall
Chillingworth, Richard Davies, 4/5 Great Britain St
Connell, Mary Ann, 2 Gill Abbey St
Cotter, Samuel, 142 Barrack St
Divett, John, 87 North Main St
Hare, Thomas, 103 Barrack St
Hegarty, Daniel, 6 Paul St
Helen, Patience, 22 Douglas St
Horgan, John, 8 Great Britain St
Leaves, Rebecca, Sullivan's Quay
Looney, Michael, 84 South Main St

Lucey, Denis, 128 Shandon St
McCarthy, Felix, 145 Barrack St
McCarthy, John, 107 North Main St
Mayne, Robert, 17 Lavitt's Quay
Miller, Rebecca, 4/5 Devonshire St
Murphy, Jeremiah, 18 St Patrick's Hill
Murphy, Patrick, 124 Shandon St
Murray, Thomas, 44 Blarney St
Nicolls, Margaret, 56 Gill Abbey St
Nunan, Catherine & Sons, 97 Shandon St
O'Driscoll, Michael, 35 Nile St
Phipps, James, Mahony's Lane
Reardon, William, 37 Shandon St
Scott, Jane, 13 Pope's Quay
Sexton, Catherine, 8 Robert St
Sheehan, Eliza, Adelaide St
Sullivan, Caroline, 5 Robert St
Swan, Bellingham, 1 Cove St
Teape, Ann, 46 North Main St
Thornhill, John, 2 Bridge St
Uniake, Catherine, 13 Rutland St
Unkles, Abigail, 43 Douglas St

Derry:

Bradley, Patrick, 10 Rossville St
Coyle, Daniel, 17 Rossville St
Crosson, Bernard, 63 Rossville St
Divine, William, 5 Long tower
Gillespie, James, 21 Bridge St
Hannigan, Bernard, Bishop St and Chapel lane
Hannigan, Denis, Waterside
Lynch, Edward, 2 Castle St
McCleery, Charles, 72 Fountain St
McCready, Thomas, 47 William St
McNulty, Charles, 57 Rossville St
Reid, John, 13 Bridge St

Dublin

Anderson, Geo., 50 Marlborough St.
Booth, Henry, 141 Thomas St.
Boyle, Joseph, 80 Bride St

Boyle, Michael, 12 Phoenix St and 2/ 3 Luke St
Browne, Mary, 85 Lr Mount St
Byrne, Francis F.W., 205 Great Britain St and 31 James St
Byrne, John, 10 & 11 Lombard St
Byrne, Richard, 43 Eccles St
Byrne, Richard, 6 Talbot St
Claffey, Patrick, 65 Amiens St and 30 Nicholas St
Cummins, Gerard, 25 High St
Cummins, Patrick, 22 South Richmond St
Cunningham, James Joseph, 46/47 Summer Hill and 48A Lr Baggot St
Delany, Richard, 50 Summer Hill and 32 /33 Lr Pembroke St
Dillon, Thomas, 29 South King St
Donnelly, J. P., 67 Great Brunswick St
Egan, James W., 85 Queen St
Fannin, Thomas, 51 Marlborough St
Farrell, Patrick, 32 Great Britain St
Fay, John, 2 Moore St
Fennell, Terence, 16 Denzille St
Finlay, Michael, 34 North Brunswick St
Flanagan, William G., 108 Capel St and 85/86 Lr Coombe
Geraghty, Thomas, 4 Ardee St
Halbert, John, 72 Francis St
Halbert, Nathaniel, 35 Corn Market
Hasson, Elizabeth, 179 Great Britain St
Hayden, Edward A., 43/44 Clarendon St
Hayden, Martin, 52 Upper Dorset St
Higgins, Patrick, 81 North King St
Ivers, John, 5 Upper Stephen St
Kean, John, 77 Aungier St
Kearns, James, 129 Summer Hill and 124 Thomas St
Keogh, James, 189 Great Britain St
Keogh, Patrick, 46 South Great George's St
McLowry, Richard, 2 St. Andrew St
McNally, Laurence, 10 Moor St and 7 Upper Buckingham St
Martin, Joseph, 2 Parliament Row, 48 Fleet St and 4 Aston's Quay
Maryon, Sophia, 11 Meath St
Meredith, Margaret, 48 Cuffe St
Mulvany, John, 19 New St
Mulvany, Matthew, 6 Upper Erne St
Nolan, James, 2/3 Pembroke St
O'Brien, Peter F., 159 Church St

Plunkett, James, 98 James St, 90 Lr Camden St and 123 Upper Dorset St
Potter, William, 28/29 Talbot St
Redmond, Denis, 66 South Great George's St
Redmond, James John, 25 Mary's Abbey and 118 Upper Abbey St
Reynolds, Matthew, 1/2 Redmond's Hill
Rispin, Bernard, 24 North Anne St
Rispin, James, 9 Charlemont St
Rochfort, Patrick, 38 Townsend St
Spencer, Henry, 120-122 Lr Coombe
Tynan, Michael, 105 Upper Dorset St
Wall, Valentine, 61 Bolton St
Whelan, Peter, 12 Lr Mecklenburg St
White, James, 17 – 19 Winetavern St, and 13/14 Exchange St
White, Richard T., 21/22 Bishop St
Wilson, John, 26 Moore St

Galway:

Boyle, John T., Abbeygate St
Duggan, Dermot, Church yard
Kirwen, John, Abbeygate St
Molony, Patrick, Cross St
Power, Michael, High St
Semple, William, William St

Kilkenny:

Bacon, Edward, St. John's St
Dowling, Walter, King St
Dunphy, Charles, King St
Goss, Agnes, King St
Heffernan, Richard, Parliament St
Rafter, James, Irishtown

Limerick:

Barry, John, Cornwallis St
Benn, Francis, 13 George's Quay
Browne, Joseph John, John St
Bunton, Jane, 7 George's Quay
Delany, William, 15 & 38 Broad St
Dowling, Jeremiah, 14 Lr Catherine St
Gallagher, John, 2 Mary St

Joynt, Dudley P., Brunswick St
Kearney, James, 2 Nicholas St
Kearney, John P., 3 Mary St
Lane, Timothy, 12 Broad St
Lyttleton, James, Upper William St
Nolan, William, 3 Corn Market Row
Parker, Margaret, 6 Nelson St
Pitts, Sarah, 44 William St Bow
Rail, Michael, 8 Nicholas St
Robinson, Thomas, Boherbuoy
Ryan, John, 7 Bridge St
Ryan, Michael, 3 Broad St and 16 Mungret St
Trousdell, Ann, 10 Nelson St

Waterford:

Carroll, Patrick, 45 Ballybricken and 26 New St
Casey, Patrick, 8 Michael St
Casey, Richard, 33 John St
Coman, Daniel, 6 Stephen St
Flannigan, Ellen, 55 Ballybricken
Finn, Maurice, Mayor's Walk
Grannan, Ellen, 13 Ballybricken
Hanagan, Declan, 55 Patrick St
Maher, Thomas, 23 Stephen St
Maxwell, Anne, 62 John St
Raleigh, Richard, 30 Barrack St
Todd, Ann, 35 Michael St
Walsh, Edward, 57 Ballybricken
Walsh, William, 9 Stephen St

BIBLIOGRAPHY

LAWS:

Pawnbrokers Act 1786 (26 Geo.3, c.43 Ir).

Pawnbrokers Act 1788 (28 Geo.3, c.49 Ir).

Duties on Certain Licences, 1804 (44 Geo.3, cxxii).

Dublin Police Magistrates Act, 1808 (48 Geo.3, c.140).

An Act for the Amendment of the Laws respecting Charitable Loan Societies in Ireland, 1823.

Dublin Justices Act, 1824, (5 Geo.4, c. 02).

An Act to amend the Laws relating to Loan Societies in Ireland, 1836.

Statutory Declarations Act, 1836 (5&6 Will.4, c. 62).

Stamp Duties (Ireland) Act, 1842 (5&6 Vict., c. 82).

An Act to remove Doubts touching the Law relating to Charitable Pawn or Deposit Offices in Ireland, 1842.

A Bill to Amend the Laws Relating to Pawnbroking in Ireland, 1843.

Stamp Act, 1853 (10&17 Vict. c. 59).

Stamp Act, 1854 (17&18 Vict. c. 83).

Revenue (no.2) Act, 1864 (27 & 28 Vict. c. 56).

Local Government (Ireland) Act, 1898 (61 & 62 Vict. c. 37).

The Summary Jurisdiction (Ireland) Act, 1908 (8 Edw. 7, C. 67).

Children Act, 1908 (8 Edw. 7, c. 67).

Firearms Act, 1925 (no. 17 of 1925).

Pension Books (Prohibition of Alienation) Act, 1932.

Pawnbrokers (Divisional Auctioneers) Act, 1943 (no. 9 of 1943).

The Pawnshop Act, 1964.

Finance Act, 1965 (S.18).

Finance Act, 1980, (S.77).

Consumer Credit Act, 1995.

ENQUIRIES:

First Report of Commission of Municipal Corporations, Ireland, 1835.

Commission on the Enquiry into the Trade of Pawnbroking In Ireland, 1837/8.

Laws of Pawnbroking in Ireland Commission of Enquiry, 1867/8.

BOOKS ON PAWNBROKING, NON-FICTION:

Hudson, Kenneth, 1982, *Pawnbroking – an aspect of British social history*, London.

Lyng, Thomas, 1995, *Bankers to the people – a personal history of pawnbroking in the city of Dublin*, London.

INTERNET:

Information on the pawn industry, National Pawnbrokers Association (USA), @ http://npa.polygon.net/infopawn.html

Brief history of pawnbroking, National Pawnbrokers Association (UK),

@ http://www.hatton-gdn.co.uk/history.htm;

Fifth Lateran Council 1512-17 A.D.

@ http://www.piar.hu/councils/ecum18.htm

ARTICLES ON PAWNBROKING:

Barrington, Matthew, *1835, An address to the inhabitants of Limerick on the opening of the Mont de Piété.*

Connery, James, 1837 *An essay on charitable economy upon the loan bank system called on the continent Mont De Piété, that is, the mount or rather the heap, for the distribution of charity, being an antidote to counteract the baneful effects of pawnbroking and other rapacious systems of moneylending, in town and country which have entailed misery on the poor.*

Report of a meeting held in the city court house on Friday October 28th 1836, for the purpose of explaining the objects of the Mont De Piété or Charitable Pawn Office and the intended system of management., Limerick 1836.

Crowley, Sean, 1988, 'Pawnbroking in Cork', *Middle Parish Chronicle*, Cork.

Dalton, Martin, 1947, 'Monday is pawnday', *The Bell*, Aug. 1947, pp 46-50.

Duffy, Paul, 'A Limerick pawnshop farthing', 1983, *North Munster Antiquarian Journal*, Vol XXV, pp 73/4.

MacL. W., 'Pawnbroking in Limerick', *The Old Limerick Journal* 1982, p.16/17.

O'Donnell, Peadar, 1942, 'People and pawnshops', *The Bell*, Dec. 1942, pp 206-

208.

Raymond, James Raymond, 1978, 'Pawnbrokers and pawnbroking in Dublin', *1830-1870*, *Dublin Historical Record*, Vol. XXXII, Dec.1978- Sept. 1979, pp.15-26.

Ryan, P.J., 1981, 'Poverty and pawnshops', The *Old Limerick Journal*, p.10/11.

GENERAL WORKS, NON-FICTION:

Andrews, Andrew, 1987, *Collins thematic dictionary of quotations*, London.

Ayling, Stanley, 1972, *George the Third*, London.

Sir Matthew Barrington, 1788-1861 The Old Limerick Journal, Barrington's Edition, no.24, 1988, pp. 11-18.

Barrington family papers, Glenstal Abbey, Limerick.

Barrow, G.L., *The emergence of the Irish banking system, 1820-1845*, Dublin.

Bassett's Directories

Boddy, Martin, 1980, *The building societies*, London .

Bourke, Austin, 1993, *The visitation of God? – the potato and the Great Irish Famine*, Dublin.

British Parliamentary Papers relating to the relief of distress during the Great Famine in Ireland

Cameron, Charles A., 1904, *How the poor live*, Dublin.

Casey, Michael, *A river of love - Frederick Ozanam and the Society of St Vincent De Paul*, The Columba Press.

Caulfield, Richard, 1876, *The Council Book of the Corporation of the City of Cork, from 1609 to 1643 and from 1690 to 1800*.

Chubb, Basil, 1971, *The government and politics of Ireland*, Oxford Press.

Cleary, Pat and O'Regan, Philip, (eds), 1995, *Dear Old Skibbereen – a glimpse of conditions in this town during the Great Irish Famine*.

Cleugh, James, 1975, *The Medici, a tale of fifteen generations*, London.

Conlan, Patrick, OFM, 1988 *Franciscan Ireland*, Dublin.

Cooney, Dudley Levistone, 2001, *The Methodists in Ireland*.

Cork Constitution Newspaper 19/2/1828, 15/7/1828, 7/1/1830, 2/2/1830.

Cork Post Office Directories

Cronin, Maura, 1994, *Country, class or craft? – the politicisation of the skilled artisan in nineteenth century Cork*, Cork University Press.

Crosbie, Paddy, 1981, *Your dinner's poured out!*, Dublin.

Cullen, Mary and Luddy, Maria, 1995, *Women, power and consciousness in nineteenth century Ireland*, Dublin.

Daly, Mary E., 1984, *Dublin, the deposed capital – a social and economic history, 1860 -1914*, Cork University Press.

Daryl, Philippe,1888, *Ireland's disease*, London.

De Lataocnayne, *A Frenchman's walk through Ireland, 1796-7*, translated by John Stevenson, 1917, re-printed 1984, Dublin.

Dickson, David (ed), 1987, *The Gorgeous Mask – Dublin 1700-1850*, Trinity history workshop, Dublin.

Dillon, T.W.T., 1945, *Slum clearance: past and future, Studies, an Irish quarterly review of letters, philosophy and science*, Vol, XXXIV, March, 1945, Dublin.

Farley, Desmond, 1964, *Social Insurance and Social Assistance in Ireland*, Institute of Public Administration, Dublin.

Faulkner, Anselm, OFM, 1978 OFM, *Liber Dubliniensis – chapter documents of the Irish Franciscans, 1719-1875*, Dublin.

Foley, John, 1993, *The Guinness Encyclopedia of Signs and Symbols*, London.

Forster, William, *Report to the Central Relief Committee during the Great Famine. Freeman's Journal*, 5/6/1840.

Gage, John, 1968, *Life in Italy at the time of the Medici*, London.

Gallagher, Thomas, 1982, *Paddy's lament – Ireland, 1846-47, prelude to hatred*, Dublin.

Goodbody, Rob, 1995 *A suitable channel - Quaker relief in the Great Famine*, Wicklow.

Guys Directories.

Hall, F.G, 1949, *Bank of Ireland, 1783-1946*, Dublin.

Hall, Anna Maria and Samuel Carter, *Hall's Ireland – Mr & Mrs Hall's Tour of 1840*, London 1841.

Hansen, Valerie, 1995 *Negotiating daily life in traditional China - how ordinary people used contracts, 600-1400*, Yale University Press.

Henchion, Richard, 1986, *Henchion's Cork Centenary Remembrancer, 1887-1987*, Cork.

Hoppen, K Theodore, 1984 *Elections, politics and society in Ireland, 1832-1885*, Oxford.

Hyman, Louis, 1972, *The Jews of Ireland from the earliest times to the year 1910*.

Inglis, Henry D.,1838, *A journey throughout Ireland during the spring, summer and autumn of 1834*, London.

Irish Crisis of 1879-80 – Proceedings of the Dublin Mansion House Relief Committee, 1880, 1881, Dublin.

Kearns, Kevin C., 1994, *Dublin tenement life – an oral history,* Dublin.

Kearns, Kevin C., 1996, *Stoneybatter – Dublin's inner urban village,* Dublin.

Kearns, Kevin C., 1996, *Dublin pub life & lore – an oral history,* Dublin.

Kelly, Fergus, 1988, *A guide to early Irish law,* Dublin Institute for Advanced Studies.

Keogh, Dermot, 1998, *Jews in twentieth-century Ireland,* Cork University Press.

Lenihan, Maurice, 1866, *The history of Limerick,* reprinted in 1991, Cork.

Lindsay, Deirdre, 1990, *Dublin's oldest charity – the Sick and Indigent Roomkeepers Society, 1790-1990,* Dublin.

Massy, Godfrey, *Memoirs of the Famine years in Bruff, The Old Limerick Journal Famine Edition,* no.32, 1995, pp. 92-96.

Mooney, Fr Canice OFM, 'The Franciscans in County Mayo', *Galway Archaeological Society Journal,* p.42-69, 1958/9.

Moorman, John, 1968 *A history of the Franciscan Order from its origins to the year 1517,* Oxford.

Morton, H.V., 1969 *A traveller in Southern Italy,* London.

Murphy, Edward, 1978 *The MacMillan Treasury of Relevant Quotations,* London.

Murphy, Maura, 'The working classes of nineteenth century Cork', *Cork Historical & Archaeological Society,* 1980.

Murphy, Nancy, and O'Brien, Fiona (Eds), *More of Nenagh's Yesterdays,* 1997, Tipperary.

McCarthy Collins, Charles, 1880, *The law and practice of banking in Ireland,* London.

McLoughlin, Adrian, 19818, *Streets of Ireland,* Dublin.

Nas na Riogh – from Poorhouse Road to the Fairy Flax, an illustrated history of Naas, Naas Local History Group, 1990.

New Catholic Encyclopedia, 1967, Catholic University of America, Washington.

O'Brien, George, 1918, *The economic history of Ireland in the eighteenth century,* London.

O'Brien, George, 1919, *The economic history of Ireland in the seventeenth century,* London.

O'Brien, Joseph V., 1982, *Dear, dirty old Dublin – a city in distress, 1899-1916,* University of California Press.

O'Connell, K.H., 1950, *The population of Ireland, 1750-1845,* Oxford.

O'Connor, John, 1995, *The Workhouses of Ireland – the fate of Ireland's poor,* Dublin.

O Croinin, Daibhi, 2000, *The Songs of Elizabeth Cronin, Irish Traditional Singer,*

Dublin.

O Dwyer, Barry W., (trans.), 1982, *Stephen of Lexington, letters from Ireland, 1228-1229*, Cistercian Fathers Series Number 28, Michigan.

O Grada, Cormac, 1988, *Ireland before and after the Famine – explorations in economic history, 1800- 1925*, Manchester University Press.

O Grada, Cormac (ed.), 1997, *Famine 150 Commemorative Lecture Series*, Dublin

O'Rahilly, Alfred, 1941, *Money*, Cork University Press.

O'Sullivan, M.D., 1962, *Italian merchant bankers in Ireland in the thirteenth century*, Dublin.

Oxford Dictionary of Etymology.

Pigots Directories.

Rich, E.E., and Wilson, C.H. (eds), *Cambridge Economic History fo Europe*, Vol. V, 1997, Cambridge.

Robins, Joseph, 1980, *The lost children: a study of charity children in Ireland, 1700-1900*, Institute of Public Administration, Dublin.

Robinson, David, 1985, *Chaplin, his life and art*, London.

Roth, Cecil, 1946, *The history of the Jews of Italy*, The Jewish Publication Society of America.

Slaters Directories.

Spufford, Peter, 1988, *Money and it's use in Medieval Europe*, Cambridge University Press.

Swords, Liam, 1999, *In their own words; the Famine in North Connacht 1845-49*, Dublin.

Thackeray, William Makepeace, 1843, *The Irish Sketchbook, 1842*, reprinted 1985, Belfast.

Tierney, Mark, 1995, *Glenstal Abbey*, Limerick.

Treacy, Brendan, 1999, *All our Nenagh's Yesterdays*, Tipperary.

Tuckey, Francis, 1837, *Cork Remembrancer*, reprinted 1980, Cork.

Walsh, Larry, 'Vincent De Paul Society, Limerick, and the Famine', *The Old Limerick Journal, Famine Edition*, no. 32, 1995.

Woodham-Smith, Cecil, 1962, *The Great Hunger*, New York.